英語でかんたん和食
Japanese HOME COOKING
with MASTER CHEF MURATA

英語でかんたん和食

Japanese HOME COOKING
with MASTER CHEF MURATA

著・村田吉弘

写真・齋藤 明

講談社

CONTENTS
目次

Introduction
はじめに……8

Using This Book／Conversions
本書の使い方／単位換算表……12

CHAPTER 1

Salads
あえもの
13

Green Beans with Sesami Sauce
いんげんのごまあえ……14

Fava Beans with Sweet Tofu Sauce
空豆の白あえ……16

Spinach with Peanut Sauce
ほうれん草のピーナツあえ……18

Daikon Radish with *Wasabi*-Soy Dressing
大根のわさび醤油あえ……20

Onion and Crispy Bacon Salad
たまねぎとカリカリベーコンのあえもの……22

Sauces 1   *Wasabi*-Mayo Sauce / Soy-Sesame Sauce
たれ1　わさびマヨネーズだれ／ごまだれ
24

CHAPTER 2

Sautéed Dishes
焼きもの
25

Beef Teriyaki
牛肉の照り焼き……26

Tofu Teriyaki
豆腐の照り焼き……28

Salmon Teriyaki
鮭の照り焼き……30

Pan-Grilled Skewered Chicken
焼き鳥……32

Sautéed Pork with Ginger and Tomato
豚肉のトマトしょうが焼き……34

Rolled Omelet
巻き卵……36

Grilled Eggplant in Sauce
焼きなすの煮びたし……38

Oil temperature
油の温度
40

CHAPTER 3 — Deep-Fried Dishes
揚げもの   *41*

Shrimp Tempura
海老の天ぷら……*42*

Kakiage Tempura
野菜のかき揚げ……*44*

Deep-Fried Oysters
かきフライ……*46*

Japanese Pork Cutlets
とんかつ……*48*

Deep-Fried Marinated Chicken Breast
鶏のから揚げ……*50*

Deep-Fried Cod
たらのから揚げ……*52*

Deep-Fried Tofu
揚げだし豆腐……*54*

Chicken Wings Escabeche
鶏の南蛮漬け……*56*

Sauces 2 Tempura Dipping Sauce — *58*
たれ2　天つゆ

CHAPTER 4 — Steamed Dishes
蒸しもの   *59*

Sake-Steamed Clams
あさりの酒蒸し……*60*

Steamed Vegetables with Peanut Butter Dressing
蒸し野菜のピーナツバターだれ……*62*

Steamed Egg Custard
茶碗蒸し……*64*

Steamed Salmon with Tofu and Mushrooms
鮭と豆腐のきのこ蒸し……*66*

Dashi 1 Easy *Dashi* / Extra-Rich *Dashi* — *68*
だし1　簡易だし／本格だし

CHAPTER 5 — Simmered Dishes
煮もの   *69*

Braised Beef and Potatoes
肉じゃが……*70*

Simmered Napa Cabbage and Pork Slices
豚肉と白菜の煮もの……*72*

Kabocha Squash and Bacon Stew
かぼちゃとベーコンの煮もの……74

Sweet-and-Sour Chicken Wings
手羽先のワインビネガー煮……76

Simmered Calamari and Daikon Radish
いかと大根の煮もの……78

Ginger Mackerel
さばのしょうが煮……80

Kimpira
きんぴら……82

Potato Kimpira with Bacon
じゃがいもとベーコンのきんぴら……84

Chicken and Vegetable Stew
筑前煮……86

Dashi 2 Chicken and Dried Tomato Broth — 88
だし2　鶏とドライトマトのだし

CHAPTER 6 Hot Pots — 89
鍋もの

Sukiyaki
すき焼き……90

Shabu-Shabu Hot Pot
しゃぶしゃぶ……92

Chicken Meatball Hot Pot
鶏だんご鍋……94

Salmon and Miso Hot Pot
鮭の味噌鍋……96

Rice 1 Cooked Rice — 98
ご飯1　ご飯の炊き方

CHAPTER 7 Rice and Noodles — 99
ご飯と麺

Marinated Tuna on Rice
まぐろの漬け丼……100

Chicken and Mushroom Rice
鶏肉とマッシュルームの混ぜご飯……102

Smoked Salmon, Butter, and Soy Sauce on Rice
スモークサーモンのバター醤油丼……104

Chicken and Egg on Rice
親子丼……106

Fried Rice
炒飯……108

Sushi Rice Bowl
ちらし寿司……110

Sushi Hand-Roll with lettuce
手巻き寿司……112

Tuna-Mayo Rice Balls
ツナマヨネーズおにぎり……114

Seared Rice Balls with Bacon Soy Sauce
ベーコン入り焼きおにぎり……116

Soba Noodles with Sweet Soy Sauce
かけそば……118

Chicken and Onion Noodle Soup
鶏ねぎそば……120

Fried Noodles
焼きそば……122

Beef Noodle Soup
肉うどん……124

Rice 2   Vinegared Sushi Rice — 126
ご飯2   寿司飯

CHAPTER 8

Soups
椀もの

127

Egg and Bacon Soup
ベーコン入りかきたま汁……128

Chicken and Tofu Soup
鶏の豆腐汁……130

Clam and *Miso* Soup
あさりの味噌汁……132

Pork and Root Vegetable Soup
豚汁……134

Glossary
食材メモ……136

Index
さくいん……140

INTRODUCTION

This book is for anyone who has ever wanted to make Japanese food, but doesn't know where to start. Most of the recipes in this book require no special ingredients or unusual equipment. I wanted to provide recipes that use ingredients found at an ordinary supermarket in America.

In fact, Japanese cooking is really not that exotic. You probably have a bottle of soy sauce in your pantry. Soy sauce, essential to Japanese cooking, is made by steaming soybeans and roasted wheat into a mash, then fermenting the mash until it develops a rounded, meaty flavor. With soy sauce and sugar you can make authentic teriyaki sauce, and then all you have to do is grill or sauté beef, salmon, tofu, or any other ingredient you wish, and baste it with the sauce to make a satisfying dish.

Also, I have chosen recipes that do not strictly call for *dashi*, a basic fish stock made from dried bonito and *kombu* kelp. Most of the soups, simmered dishes, and hot pots call for chicken broth that can be bought at the supermarket in the West. Even in Japan we often use chicken broth, usually in powder form, for many of these dishes. (For cooks who want to try it, I have included a method for making dashi and a few recipes that use it.)

The recipes in this book reflect authentic Japanese home cooking. I learned them from my father, my mother, and my grandmother. A few I picked up outside my home, when I tried something I thought was good and asked the cook for the recipe. I've put the recipes in my own words, but the dishes are all familiar favorites that Japanese know from their mothers' cooking.

At my restaurant, Kikunoi, in Kyoto, Japan, I serve *kaiseki* cuisine, which has its roots in the Buddhist monastic tea ceremony and has been continuously refined for centuries down to the present day. However, I have long believed that the food we ate at home as children, lovingly prepared by our mothers, is the truest and best cooking we know. Mothers adjust for each child's tastes and season with the utmost attention. It is the greatest effort a cook can put forth. As a professional chef, I must compete with other restaurants to provide outstanding meals, but I'm happiest when I know that I am cooking for a person who will truly enjoy what they eat.

はじめに

　この本は海外で「和食を作ってみたいけれど、何から始めればよいかわからない」という方のためのものです。特別な材料も道具も必要ありません。アメリカのスーパーマーケットで手に入るような、ごく普通の食材を使った料理ばかりです。

　家庭で作る和食は凝ったものではありません。海外であっても、醤油ぐらいはお持ちの方も多いのではないでしょうか？　和食に欠かせない醤油は、蒸した大豆と炒って砕いた小麦粉を混ぜ合わせて作られます。混ぜたあとで時間をかけて発酵・熟成させ、まろやかでうま味たっぷりの醤油ができあがるのです。醤油と砂糖があれば、本格的な照り焼きのたれを作ることができ、そのたれをかけながら牛肉、鮭、豆腐などお好みの食材を焼くだけで、満足のいく一皿になります。

　この本のなかでは、かつおぶしや昆布でだしをとる手間もかけません。大半の椀もの、煮もの、鍋ものは欧米で市販されているチキンスープを使っています。日本でも顆粒のチキンスープはよく使われます（ご希望の方のためにだしのとり方などものせましたので、ご参考にしてください）。

　ご紹介した料理は、長い間日本人の食卓にのぼってきたものです。ほとんどは祖母や両親から習ったものですが、外で味わって料理法を訊き、参考にしたものもいくつかあります。レシピは私自身のものですが、日本人なら母の味としてなじみ深いものばかりです。

　京都にある私の料亭〈菊乃井〉では、懐石料理をお出しします。懐石料理は禅寺の修業僧の茶事に始まり、今日にいたるまで長年かけて格式ある料理に研ぎ澄まされてきました。ですが、私自身は子供のころに母親が愛情をこめて作ってくれた家庭料理こそ、最高の料理だと思っています。母親はそれぞれの子供に合うように味つけを変えます。そういった心づかいが料理を輝かせるのです。プロの料理人として際立った料理をお出しする務めがありますが、召し上がる方が本当に喜んでくださる料理を作っているときがいちばん幸せかもしれません。

Through the Japanese Culinary Academy, a nonprofit organization dedicated to teaching and promoting Japanese cuisine, I have invited many chefs from the West to Japan, and I am often invited to other countries. I think that all chefs want to focus on their customers' needs, especially by providing more health-conscious meals, which is now a global trend. It seems that the most accomplished chefs are the ones most eager to learn something, even just a little bit, about healthy techniques and ingredients from Japanese cuisine.

The main reason for the healthiness of Japanese cuisine is because we don't rely on fat and oil for flavor, but instead try to bring out the natural *umami* in foods. Many ordinary foods have umami, the "fifth taste," which is different from saltiness or sweetness. Aged cheese and beef contain a lot of umami, as do ripe tomatoes and good wine. The dense savor of root vegetables or the subtle sweetness of raw fish are further examples of umami. Even types of salt vary in this respect: refined salt is just plain salty, but we Japanese prefer the more rounded flavor of natural sea salt because it has umami.

Of course, anyone can detect the taste of umami, even if they don't have a word for it. It is said that milk consists of sweetness, richness, and umami, which means that as mammals we are all programmed from birth to crave foods high in sugar, fat, and amino acids that provide umami. But in Japan, Buddhist strictures prevented us from eating meat or animal fats until the late nineteenth century; and refined sugar and other sweeteners were until recently too expensive for most Japanese to use. Therefore, Japanese cuisine has developed in a very different way from Western and other Asian cuisines: we satisfy our biological need for the flavors of milk by focusing on umami rather than fats and sweeteners.

We all wish to be healthier, but if you always dine out or buy takeout food, you'll never even get started. By cooking the same recipe repeatedly, and sometimes cooking for others (and sometimes making mistakes), the dishes you make will improve and you will cook with more confidence. As you cook more, you can add your own variations, widening your repertoire. Nothing will change if you don't challenge yourself. So, why not begin cooking healthy food at home? I assure you that with this book, you can cook Japanese food quickly and easily and develop a close feeling for the cuisine. It is my pleasure to help you, even if only a little bit, to lead a healthier life and make yourself and your loved ones happier.

Yoshihiro Murata

日本料理の教育・発展を目的とする特定非営利活動法人〈日本料理アカデミー〉の活動を通し、これまで欧米から多くの料理人の方々を招聘し、私も多くの国を訪れました。すべての料理人はお客様の要望を受け、世界的な傾向として特に健康を意識した料理へと移行しています。大なり小なり、和食の食材や技を取り入れて成功した料理人も数多くいます。

　和食が健康的なのは、味つけをバターや油に頼らず、素材のうま味を自然に引き出すところにあります。熟成したチーズ、牛肉、トマトやワインのように、食べ物には塩気や甘さとは異なる"第五の味覚"「うま味」が備わっています。根菜類の力強さや刺身のかすかな甘みも、うま味の一種です。塩の種類というのも関わりがあり、工場生産された塩には塩辛さしか感じませんが、日本人は自然の海塩にあるまろやかなうま味を感じ、好んできました。

　うま味という言葉を知らなくても、感じることはできます。牛乳には甘味、風味、うま味があると言われています。哺乳類は生まれたときから、砂糖、脂肪、うま味の素となるアミノ酸を欲するように作られているのです。しかし日本では、仏教思想によって19世紀後半まで肉食は大衆には広まっていませんでした。砂糖や甘味料も一般的に高価だったので、和食は西欧料理や他のアジア諸国の料理とはだいぶ異なる形で発展してきました。動物脂肪や甘味料の代わりに、素材のうま味をいかに引き出すかということを考えてきたのです。

　誰もが健康を願いますが、外食やテイクアウトばかりではかないません。失敗を重ねながらも、自分や他の人のために何度も同じ料理を作ることで上達し、自信も付きます。料理する習慣が身に付けば、自然にレパートリーも広がります。始めなければ、何も変わりません。ご自宅で健康的な和食を作ってみませんか？　この本があれば、手早く簡単に作ることができ、和食が身近に感じられるでしょう。少しでも、健康や、皆様とその大切な方々の喜びに役立つことができれば、こんなにうれしいことはありません。

USING THIS BOOK 本書の使い方

This is a Japanese-English bilingual edition of *Japanese Home Cooking with Master Chef Murata*. Some recipes as well as the sequence and layout of content differ from the original version.

Standard U.S. measures are used throughout this book; the metric conversions in parentheses are also in accordance with U.S. standards.
- For fluid measures, 1 cup = 240 ml (rounded up from 236.59 ml).
- For weights, 1 ounce = 30 g (rounded up from 28.349 g).

Please use the conversion table below as a guide.

Please choose low-sodium or sodium-free chicken broth if available.

Microwave cooking times are for a 500-watt microwave oven. Lower-powered ovens will need longer cooking times.

本書は、*Japanese Home Cooking with Master Chef Murata* の対訳版です。収録してある料理、順番、デザインなど変更している部分もあります。

分量表記（英文）およびメートル法表記はアメリカで一般的な基準に従っています。
- 液体の分量　1カップ＝240ml (236.59mlを切り上げ)
- 重さ　1オンス＝30g (28.349gを切り上げ)

下記の単位換算表をご参考にしてください。

チキンスープは、ナトリウムを含まないか少ないものをなるべくお使いください。

電子レンジは500ワットを基準にしています。ワット数が低いときはレンジにかける時間を長くしてください。

CONVERSIONS 単位換算表

Volume 容量

Metric メートル法	USA アメリカ
5 ml	1 teaspoon
15 ml	1 tablespoon
50 ml	3 tablespoons + 1 teaspoon
60 ml	1/4 U.S.cup
80 ml	1/3 U.S cup
100 ml	1/3 U.S.cup + 4 teaspoons
240 ml	U.S.1 cup
400 ml	U.S. 1 2/3 cups
480 ml	U.S. 2 cups = 1 pint
1000 ml (1 L)	U.S. 4 cups = 2 pints = 1 quart

Weight 重量

Grams グラム	USA アメリカ
10 g	1/3 ounce
15 g	1/2 ounce
20 g	2/3 ounce
30 g	1 ounce
50 g	1 2/3 ounces
100 g	3 1/2 ounces
150 g	5 ounces
200 g	7 ounces

Length 長さ

Metric メートル法	USA アメリカ
3 mm	1/8 inch
6 mm	1/4 inch
1.25 cm	1/2 inch
2.5 cm	1 inch
5 cm	2 inches
6.25 cm	2 1/2 inches
7.5 cm	3 inches
10 cm	4 inches

Temperature 温度

Celsius (C°) 摂氏	Fahrenheit (°F) 華氏
120 °C	250 °F
130 °C	275 °F
150 °C	300 °F
160 °C	325 °F
170 °C	340 °F
180 °C	350 °F
190 °C	375 °F
200 °C	390 °F

Chapter 1

Salads

あえもの 【*Aemono*】

The salads in this section are just examples; once you grasp the basic sauce and dressing recipes introduced here, you can easily create your own *aemono* using your favorite ingredients.

ここでご紹介したものは一例にすぎません。
基本のあえ衣をもとに、
お好みの食材でさまざまなものを作ることができます。

GREEN BEANS WITH SESAME SAUCE

Seasonal vegetables dressed with ground sesame seeds is a classic recipe with its roots in vegan Buddhist monastic cooking (known as *shojin* cuisine).

INGREDIENTS

Serves Two

6 oz. (170 g) young green beans
2 qts. (2 L) water for cooking green beans
1 tsp salt
Sesame dressing:
- 1 Tbsp toasted sesame seeds
- 1 tsp soy sauce
- 1 tsp sugar

1 Bring the water and salt to a boil in large pot. Rinse the green beans, remove the stem ends and cut into about 1 ½ in. (4 cm) long pieces. Cook in the boiling water until tender but still crisp. Shock in cold water and drain well.

2 Chop the sesame seeds with a knife (if making a large batch you can use a food processor) and combine with the soy sauce and sugar in a medium bowl to make the sesame sauce. Dress the green beans with the sauce and mound on a serving dish.

いんげんのごまあえ

2人分
いんげん　170g
［あえ衣］
- いりごま　大さじ1
- 醤油　小さじ1
- 砂糖　小さじ1

1 たっぷりの湯を沸かし、塩を加える。いんげんは硬い両端部分を切り落とし、約4cmに切る。歯ごたえが少し残る程度にゆでる。冷水にとってから水気をよくきる。

2 包丁で叩いたいりごまに（量が多い場合は、フードプロセッサーを使ってもよい）、醤油と砂糖と混ぜてあえ衣を作る。いんげんを加え、全体をあえて器にこんもりと盛る。

FAVA BEANS
WITH SWEET TOFU SAUCE

This tofu dressing also goes well with steamed shucked clams, cubes of grilled salmon, and even fruits like persimmon.

INGREDIENTS

Serves Two

7 oz. (200 g) fresh fava beans, removed from pods but not skinned
2 qts. (2 L) water for cooking fava beans
1 tsp salt
Sweet tofu dressing:
- 1/3 block (4 oz. / 120 g) firm tofu
- 1 tsp peanut butter
- 1 tsp sugar
- 1 tsp soy sauce

1 Bring the water and salt to a boil in large pot. Cook the fava beans in the boiling water until tender. Shock in cold water, drain, and slip the beans out of their skins. Set aside.

2 Wrap the block of tofu in several paper towels, place on a microwave-safe dish, and microwave for 1 minute in order to remove water from the tofu. Remove the paper towels.

3 Place the sugar, soy sauce and peanut butter in a medium bowl, add the tofu, and combine well by crushing the tofu and mixing with a rubber spatula. Add the fava beans to the bowl and toss with the tofu dressing.

空豆の白あえ

2人分
空豆　200g（さやから出す。薄皮はむかない）
[あえ衣]
- 豆腐（木綿）　1/3丁（120g）
- ピーナツバター　小さじ1
- 砂糖　小さじ1
- 醤油　小さじ1

1 たっぷりの湯を沸かし、塩を加える。空豆をやわらかくなるまでゆでる。冷水にとってから水気をよくきり、薄皮をむく。

2 豆腐を数枚のキッチンペーパーに包んで耐熱皿にのせ、電子レンジに1分かけて水気をきる。ペーパーをはずす。

3 砂糖、醤油、ピーナツバターをよく混ぜる。豆腐を加え、へらなどでつぶしながらよくなじませる。空豆を入れて全体を軽くあえる。

SPINACH WITH PEANUT SAUCE

Sautéing spinach immediately after rinsing it leaves just the right amount of liquid in the cooked spinach to make a dressing with the peanut butter.

INGREDIENTS

Serves Two

1 bunch fresh spinach, about 6 oz. (170 g)

Peanut dressing:
- 2 Tbsp salted peanut butter
- 1 tsp sugar

¼ cup (40 g) unsalted roasted peanuts, crushed, for topping

1 Trim off the roots of the spinach if attached, rinse in cold water and cut into 2 in. (5 cm) pieces. Heat a non-stick frying pan, add the spinach and cook over medium-low heat, stirring from time to time, until the stems of the spinach are tender but still crisp. Turn off the heat and leave in the pan until cooled to room temperature.

2 Combine the peanut butter and sugar in a medium bowl. Dress the spinach with the sauce and mound on a serving dish. Sprinkle with the crushed peanuts.

Put the peanuts in a plastic bag and crush with a rolling pin.

The water from the spinach thins the sauce to the right consistency.

ほうれん草のピーナツあえ

2人分

ほうれん草　1束 (170 g)
[あえ衣]
- ピーナツバター（有塩）大さじ2
- 砂糖　小さじ1

ピーナツ（無塩。砕いたもの）40 g

1 ほうれん草は根元の硬い部分を切り落とす。洗って5cmに切る。フッ素樹脂加工のフライパンを熱し、弱火から中火でときどきゆすりながら、ほうれん草を歯ごたえが少し残る程度に炒める。火を止め、室温になるまで冷ます。

2 ピーナツバターと砂糖を混ぜる。ほうれん草を入れ、味がなじむように全体をあえて器にこんもりと盛る。砕いたピーナツを散らす。

ピーナツはポリ袋に入れ、上からめん棒で叩いて砕く。

ほうれん草から出る水分で味が薄まり、ちょうどよい濃さになる。

DAIKON RADISH WITH *WASABI*-SOY DRESSING

Thinly cut *daikon* can be eaten just as it is, shredded and tossed with dressing, but here I added *kamaboko*, a kind of fish cake, to give the dish a deeper flavor.

INGREDIENTS

Serves Two

- 3 in. (7.5 cm) length *daikon* radish, peeled (about 8 oz. / 230 g)
- 1/2 log (about 5 oz. / 140 g) *kamaboko* (or 12 *kanikama* imitation crab legs, thawed if frozen)
- 1/2 stick celery, chopped

Wasabi-soy dressing:
- 2 Tbsp *wasabi* paste
- 1 1/3 Tbsp soy sauce
- 1 1/3 Tbsp lemon juice
- 2 tsp sugar
- 1/2 Tbsp toasted sesame seeds

1 Peel the daikon and cut into thin sticks. Cut the kamaboko into thin sticks about the same size as the daikon sticks. (If using imitation crab legs, roughly shred them by hand. If the thawed meat is too watery, simply pat dry with a paper towel.) Combine the daikon, kamaboko, and celery in a large bowl and transfer to a serving bowl.

2 Combine all dressing ingredients in a small bowl. Just before serving, pour the dressing over the vegetables and toss.

大根のわさび醤油あえ

2人分

- 大根（皮をむく） 230 g
- かまぼこ 1/2本（140 g）
  （または、かにかまぼこ 12本）
- セロリ（みじん切り） 1/2本分

［わさび醤油だれ］
- わさび 大さじ2
- 醤油 大さじ1 1/3
- レモン汁 大さじ1 1/3
- 砂糖 小さじ2
- いりごま 大さじ1/2

1 大根とかまぼこは、同じぐらいの長さの細い棒状に切る（かにかまぼこは、食べやすく手で裂く。冷凍のものは解凍し、水っぽい場合は、キッチンペーパーに包んで軽く叩いて水気をきる）。大根、かまぼこ、セロリを混ぜて器に盛る。

2 たれの材料を混ぜる。食べる直前にたれをかけ、全体をあえる。

ONION AND CRISPY BACON SALAD

Onion salad makes a good side dish for grilled meats, and eating raw sliced onion is a refreshing way to clean the palate during a meal.

INGREDIENTS

Serves Two

1 onion (sweet, red, or yellow), peeled and thinly sliced
1 cup (33 g) lightly packed washed and trimmed radish sprouts
2 cups (80 g) lightly packed baby salad greens, washed
2 oz. (60 g) sliced bacon (about 2 regular slices), chopped

Peanut and *wasabi*-mayo dressing:
- 1 Tbsp salted peanut butter
- 1 Tbsp *wasabi* paste
- 1 Tbsp mayonnaise
- 1 Tbsp soy sauce
- 1 Tbsp lemon juice
- 1 Tbsp chopped scallion
- 2 tsp toasted sesame seeds

1 If using an ordinary strong-tasting onion such as a yellow onion, soak the slices in cold water for about 20 minutes, drain, and blot dry.

2 Cook the bacon in a frying pan over medium-low heat until crisp, about 10 minutes. Transfer to paper towels to drain.

3 Mix all dressing ingredients together in a small bowl. Arrange the onion, radish sprouts, and baby salad greens in a salad bowl and top with the bacon. Just before eating, pour the dressing over the vegetables and toss.

たまねぎとカリカリベーコンのあえもの

2人分
たまねぎ
　（または紫たまねぎ）　1個
かいわれ大根　33g
ベビーリーフ　80g
ベーコンスライス　60g
［ピーナツとわさびマヨネーズだれ］
　ピーナツバター（有塩）
　　大さじ1
　わさび　大さじ1
　マヨネーズ　大さじ1
　醤油　大さじ1
　レモン汁　大さじ1
　細ねぎのみじん切り　大さじ1
　いりごま　小さじ2

1 たまねぎを薄切りにする（普通のたまねぎの場合は、薄切りした後で水に20分ほどさらし、水気をきる）。キッチンペーパーなどで水分をふきとる。

2 細切りにしたベーコンを弱火から中火で、カリッとするまで10分ほど炒める。キッチンペーパーにのせて油をきる。

3 たれの材料を混ぜる。器にたまねぎ、かいわれ大根、ベビーリーフを入れ、ベーコンをのせる。食べる直前にたれをかけて全体をあえる。

Sauces 1 / たれ 1

Here's how to make the *wasabi*-mayo sauce used on p.46 and the soy-sesame sauce on p. 48.

p.46で使用したわさびマヨネーズだれと、p48で使用したごまだれの作り方をご紹介しましょう。

WASABI-MAYO SAUCE

If this sauce has too much of a kick for you, reduce the *wasabi* to half the amount or less.

INGREDIENTS makes about 2/3 cup (160 ml)

1/4 cup (60 ml) soy sauce
1/4 cup plus 2 Tbsp (90 ml) mayonnaise
2 Tbsp *wasabi* paste
2 Tbsp sugar

Mix all ingredients together in a bowl.

SOY-SESAME SAUCE

Do not let the sauce come to a rolling boil at any point, or the cornstarch will break up and the sauce will not thicken.

INGREDIENTS makes about 1 cup (240 ml)

1 Tbsp sesame paste
3 Tbsp chicken broth
2/3 cup (160 ml) water
1 Tbsp soy sauce
1/3 cup (80 ml) Worcestershire sauce
1 1/2 Tbsp cornstarch

Combine all ingredients in a small saucepan and bring to a simmer, stirring constantly. Continue to simmer gently until the sauce thickens. If you scoop some of the sauce up with a spoon, and it drops off the spoon like pea soup, then it's the right consistency.

わさびマヨネーズだれ

わさびがききすぎるようなら、分量を減らしましょう。

できあがり 約2/3カップ

醤油　1/4カップ
マヨネーズ　1/4カップと大さじ2
わさび　大さじ2
砂糖　大さじ2

すべての材料をボウルに入れ、混ぜる。

ごまだれ

沸騰するとコーンスターチがダマになるので気を付けましょう。

できあがり 約1カップ

練りごま　大さじ1
チキンスープ　大さじ3
水　2/3カップ
醤油　大さじ1
ウスターソース　1/3カップ
コーンスターチ　大さじ1 1/2

すべての材料を小鍋に入れて煮立て、かき混ぜながら煮る。たれにとろみが付くまで煮詰める。

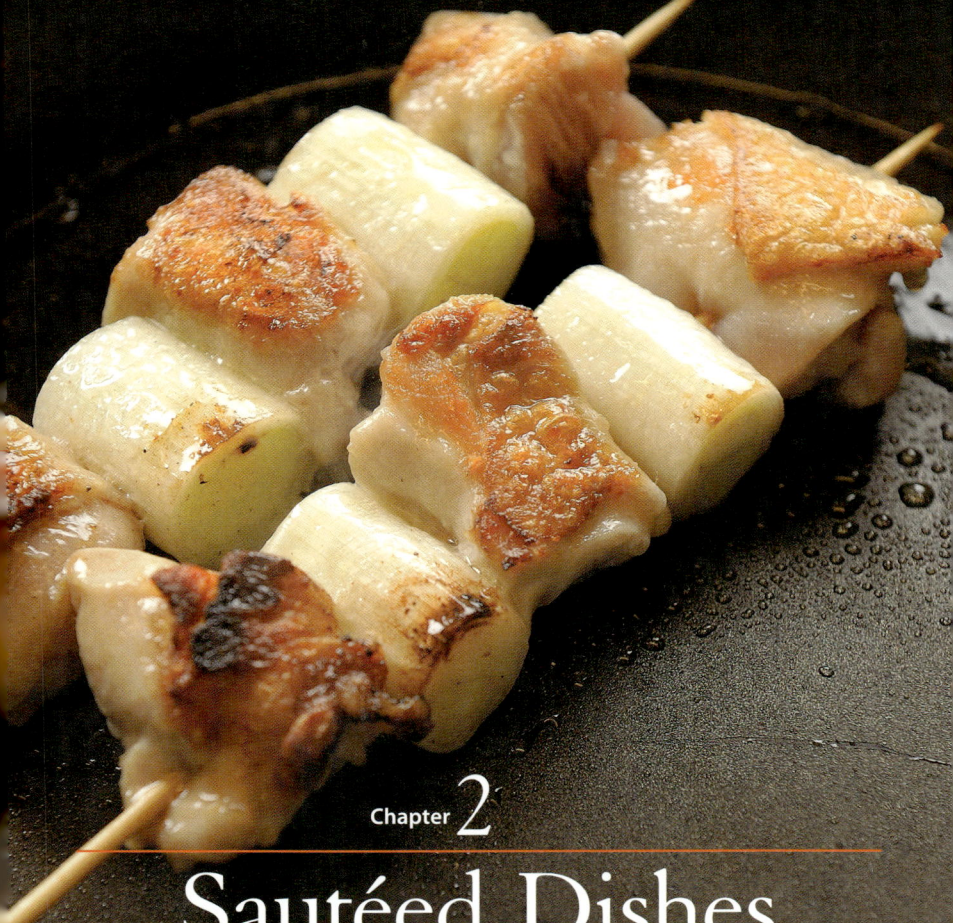

Chapter 2
Sautéed Dishes

焼きもの【Yakimono】

This section includes some popular teriyaki dishes easily made at home. They are wonderful both as everyday meals and for entertaining friends. You need only an ordinary frying pan; non-stick works best.

照り焼きをはじめ、日々の献立にもおもてなしにも役立つものばかりです。フライパン（できればフッ素樹脂加工のもの）だけで作ることができます。

BEEF TERIYAKI

Technically speaking, teriyaki is not really a sauce, but a grilling technique that uses sweetened soy sauce as a glaze. My recommendation for the best glaze is to use 1 part sugar, 2 parts soy sauce, and 4 parts *sake*.

● My recommendation for the best glaze is to use 1 part sugar, 2 parts soy sauce, and 4 parts sake.
照り焼きのたれは、砂糖、醤油、酒＝１：２：４がお勧めです。

INGREDIENTS Serves Two

2 beefsteaks, 3 1/2 oz. (100 g) each
1 Tbsp vegetable oil
Teriyaki sauce (mixed in advance):
  1 1/2 Tbsp sugar
  3 Tbsp soy sauce
  6 Tbsp *sake*
2 tsp *wasabi* paste
Slivered lemon peel
1 cup (40 g) lightly packed baby salad greens, washed and spun dry
4 florets broccoli, blanched

1 Heat a frying pan over medium-high heat, add the oil, and sear the steaks on both sides until browned. Lower the heat to medium. Add the teriyaki sauce and simmer, shaking the pan from time to time and basting the steaks with a spoon, until the sauce thickens slightly and glazes the steaks, about 4 minutes.

2 Transfer the steaks to a cutting board and cut into 1/2 in. (1.5 cm) thick slices.

3 Arrange the steak slices on a serving plate and pour the sauce from the pan over. Top with the wasabi paste and slivered lemon peel. Place the baby salad greens and broccoli on the side.

Simmer the teriyaki sauce, being careful not to scorch the pan.
フライパンを焦がさないよう、照り焼きのたれを煮詰める。

Baste the steaks from time to time to glaze them with the sauce.
ときどきたれを肉にかけ、照りを出す。

牛肉の照り焼き

2人分

牛肉（ステーキ用） 2枚（各100g）
植物油 大さじ1
[照り焼きのたれ]（合わせておく）
  砂糖 大さじ1 1/2
  醤油 大さじ3
  酒 大さじ6
わさび 小さじ2
レモンの皮（細切り） 適量
ベビーリーフ 40g
ブロッコリー 4房

1 フライパンを中火から強火に熱して油をなじませる。牛肉を入れて両面に焼き色を付ける。中火にしてたれを加えて煮立てる。ときどきフライパンをゆすり、スプーンで肉にたれを回しかけながら4分ほど煮詰めて照りを出す。

2 肉を取り出し、1.5cmに切る。

3 肉を器に盛り、たれをかける。わさびとレモンの皮をのせる。ベビーリーフと硬めにゆでたブロッコリーを添える。

TOFU TERIYAKI

This is a great way to eat tofu. Be sure to sauté the tofu until the surface is browned, so it will not break apart quite as easily.

INGREDIENTS

Serves Two

1 block firm tofu, about 12 oz. (340 g)
2 Tbsp cornstarch
1 Tbsp vegetable oil
Teriyaki sauce (mixed in advance):
- 1½ Tbsp sugar
- 3 Tbsp soy sauce
- ¼ cup plus 2 Tbsp (90 ml) *sake*

1 small, sweet pepper such as Anaheim
2 scallions, chopped
Crushed chili pepper (or *shichimi* spice powder)
1 cup (10 g) lightly packed dried bonito flakes (optional)

1 Dust the tofu with the cornstarch. Heat a large, non-stick frying pan over medium-high heat, add the oil, and sear the tofu on both sides until golden brown. Lower the heat to medium. Add the teriyaki sauce and bring to a simmer. Add the green pepper and continue to simmer, shaking the pan from time to time and basting the tofu with a spoon, until the sauce thickens and glazes the tofu, about 4 minutes.

2 Working carefully so as not to break it, transfer the tofu to a cutting board and cut into ½ in. (1.5 cm) thick slices.

3 Arrange the tofu slices and green peppers on a serving plate and pour the sauce from the pan over. Top with the chopped scallions and crushed chili pepper. Garnish with the dried bonito flakes, if desired.

豆腐の照り焼き

2人分

豆腐（木綿）　1丁（340g）
コーンスターチ　大さじ2
植物油　大さじ1
［照り焼きのたれ］（合わせておく）
- 砂糖　大さじ1½
- 醤油　大さじ3
- 酒　¼カップと大さじ2

アナハイム・ペッパー（または同様の甘唐辛子）　小1個
細ねぎ（みじん切り）　2本分
唐辛子（みじん切り。または七味唐辛子）　適量
かつおぶし（好みで）　10g

1 豆腐にコーンスターチをまぶす。フッ素樹脂加工のフライパンを中火から強火に熱して油をなじませ、豆腐の両面をこんがりと焼く。中火にしてたれを入れて煮立てる。アナハイム・ペッパーを加え、ときどきフライパンをゆすり、スプーンで豆腐にたれを回しかけながら4分ほど煮詰めて照りを出す。

2 豆腐を取り出し、1.5cmに切る。

3 豆腐とアナハイム・ペッパーを皿に盛り、煮詰めたたれをかける。細ねぎをのせ、唐辛子をふる。好みでかつおぶしを散らす。

SALMON TERIYAKI

The smokiness of the browned skin adds
an appetizing aroma to this dish.

INGREDIENTS

Serves Two

2 slices salmon, each 6 oz. (170 g)
Teriyaki sauce (mixed in advance):
- 2½ Tbsp sugar
- 3 Tbsp soy sauce
- ¼ cup plus 2 Tbsp (90 ml) *sake*

2 Tbsp cornstarch
1 Tbsp vegetable oil
1 tsp butter
Slivered lemon peel

1 Marinate the salmon in the teriyaki sauce for about 10 minutes. Remove the salmon from the marinade, blot dry, and dust with the cornstarch. Reserve the teriyaki sauce.

2 Heat the oil in a frying pan over low heat. Sauté the salmon, skin-side down, until well-browned, fragrant and crisp. Turn over and cook until the flesh side is lightly browned. Remove from heat and take off the skin. Set aside.

3 In a separate pan, heat the butter until it foams. Pour in the reserved teriyaki sauce and simmer over low heat until the sauce thickens into a glaze. Add the salmon to the pan and baste with the sauce.

4 Pour the sauce into a serving dish. Arrange the salmon on the sauce and top with the slivered lemon peel.

鮭の照り焼き

2人分

鮭　2切れ（各170g）
［照り焼きのたれ］（合わせておく）
- 砂糖　大さじ2½
- 醤油　大さじ3
- 酒　1/4カップと大さじ2

コーンスターチ　大さじ2
植物油　大さじ1
バター　小さじ1
レモンの皮（細切り）　適量

1 たれに、鮭を10分漬けておく。水気をふきとり、鮭にコーンスターチをまぶす。たれは取っておく。

2 フライパンを弱火にかけて油をなじませる。皮が付いているほうを下にして鮭を入れ、皮に焼き色が付き、香ばしく、カリッとするまで焼く。返して、身のほうも薄く焼き色が付くまで焼く。火からはずし、皮を取り除く。

3 鍋を温めてバターを溶かす。バターが泡立ってきたら、取っておいたたれを加え、弱火で煮詰めて照りを出す。鮭を鍋に入れ、たれを回しかけて焼く。

4 器に煮詰めたたれを敷き、鮭をのせる。細切りにしたレモンの皮を飾る。

PAN-GRILLED SKEWERED CHICKEN

Yakitori (grilled chicken) is popular at many Japanese eateries. It can easily be made at home in a frying pan.

INGREDIENTS

Serves Two

- 6 or more bamboo skewers
- 7 oz. (200 g) chicken thighs
- 7 oz. (200 g) chicken breast
- 1 medium green bell pepper or any sweet pepper, halved and seeded
- 2 fresh *shiitake* mushrooms, cleaned, stems removed
- ¼ onion or Japanese long onion (*naganegi*)
- 1 Tbsp vegetable oil
- Teriyaki sauce (mixed in advance):
  - 2 Tbsp sugar
  - ¼ cup (60 ml) soy sauce
  - 1 cup (240 ml) *sake*
- ½ tsp crushed chili pepper or *shichimi* spice powder (optional)

1. Cut the chicken into 1 ¼ in. (3 cm) cubes. Cut the bell pepper, mushrooms, and onion into pieces about the same size as the chicken. Thread the chicken, bell peppers, mushrooms, and onion onto skewers.

2. Heat the oil in a large frying pan over medium-low heat. Lay the skewers into the pan and cook for about 15 minutes, turning from time to time, until the chicken is nicely browned.

3. Add the teriyaki sauce to the pan and simmer, occasionally basting the skewers, until the sauce thickens and glazes the meat and vegetables, about 4 minutes.

4. Arrange the skewers on a serving platter and pour the sauce over. Serve with the crushed chili pepper and/or shichimi spice powder, if desired.

焼き鳥

2人分

竹串　6本以上
鶏もも肉　200 g
鶏胸肉　200 g
ピーマン（または甘唐辛子。半分に切り、種を取り除く）　1個
しいたけ（軸を除き、汚れをふく）　2枚
たまねぎ（または長ねぎ）　¼個
植物油　大さじ1
［照り焼きのたれ］（合わせておく）
　砂糖　大さじ2
　醤油　¼カップ
　酒　1カップ
唐辛子（みじん切り。または七味唐辛子。好みで）　小さじ½

1. 鶏肉を3 cm角に切る。ピーマン、しいたけ、たまねぎもそれぞれ鶏肉と同じぐらいの大きさに切る。鶏肉、ピーマン、しいたけを、鶏肉と野菜が交互になるように竹串に刺す。鶏肉とたまねぎも交互に竹串に刺す。

2. フライパンを弱火から中火に熱して油をなじませる。串を入れ、ときどき返しながら、両面に焼き色がつくまで15分ほど焼く。

3. 照り焼きのたれを加えて煮立てる。ときどき鶏肉と野菜にたれを回しかけながら、4分ほど煮詰めて照りを出す。

4. 串を器に盛り、たれをかける。好みで、唐辛子を添える。

SAUTÉED PORK WITH GINGER AND TOMATO

The rich aroma of soy sauce, sugar, and ginger from this dish is sure to whet your appetite.

INGREDIENTS

Serves Two

Thin-cut boneless pork loin chops, preferably from the shoulder end, about 7 oz. (200 g) total

2 Tbsp cornstarch

2 tsp vegetable oil

Teriyaki sauce (mixed in advance):
- 1½ Tbsp sugar
- 3 Tbsp soy sauce
- ¼ cup plus 2 Tbsp (90 ml) *sake*

½ regular tomato, cored and chopped

1 small knob ginger, peeled and grated

⅛ head cabbage, washed, very thinly shredded, and soaked in cold water

1 Dust the pork with cornstarch. Place a frying pan over medium-high heat, add the oil, and sear the pork on both sides until golden brown.

2 Lower the heat to medium. Add the teriyaki sauce and simmer, shaking the pan from time to time, until the sauce thickens a little, about 4 minutes. Add the tomato, bring to a simmer again, and remove from heat. Add the grated ginger and its juice.

3 Arrange the pork on a serving plate with the sauce from the pan. Drain the cabbage and serve a generous heap of it on the side.

- For the pork, thinner is better, so ask your butcher to cut the pork loin into ¼ in. (6 mm) or thinner chops.

  The shredded cabbage is refreshing and offsets the richness of the pork. No dressing is needed!

  豚肉は薄切りのほうがおいしくできます。海外では薄切り肉は手に入りにくいので、精肉店で6 mm以下に切ってもらいましょう。

  千切りのキャベツは肉のこってり感をやわらげ、後味もさっぱりとします。ドレッシングは必要ありません。

豚肉の
トマトしょうが焼き

2人分

豚薄切り肉（肩肉など）　200ｇ
コーンスターチ　大さじ2
植物油　小さじ2
［照り焼きのたれ］（合わせておく）
- 砂糖　大さじ1½
- 醤油　大さじ3
- 酒　¼カップと大さじ2

トマト（芯を除く。みじん切り）　½個
おろししょうが　1片分
キャベツ（千切りにして冷水に漬ける）　⅛個

1 豚肉にコーンスターチをまぶす。フライパンを中火から強火に熱して油をなじませる。肉の両面をこんがりと焼く。

2 中火にしてたれを加えて煮立てる。ときどきフライパンをゆすり、4分ほど煮詰める。トマトを加えて再び煮立て、火からはずす。おろししょうがと絞り汁を入れる。

3 器に豚肉をたれごと盛る。キャベツの水気をきって添える。

ROLLED OMELET

This popular Japanese omelet is rolled into a flat cylinder, allowed to cool, and sliced so that it is easy to eat with chopsticks.

Spread the eggs in the center of the foil and begin to roll.

ホイルの中央に卵を広げて巻く。

Roll the eggs securely. Tuck in both ends if the eggs come out.

卵をしっかりと巻く。はみださないよう、両端を内側に押し込む。

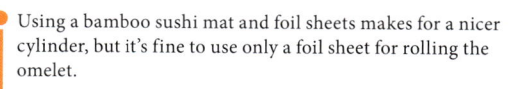

Allow to cool to room temperature to set the rolled omelet.

室温になるまで冷まし、卵を固める。

- Using a bamboo sushi mat and foil sheets makes for a nicer cylinder, but it's fine to use only a foil sheet for rolling the omelet.

  To make a sweeter style of rolled omelet, add about two tablespoons of sugar when beating the eggs.

  寿司用の竹のすのこがあると巻きやすいですが、なければアルミホイルだけでも大丈夫です。

  甘めの卵焼きにしたいときは、卵液に砂糖を大さじ2ほど加えます。

INGREDIENTS Serves Two

3 eggs
2 tsp chicken broth
3 Tbsp water
2 tsp soy sauce
1 Tbsp vegetable oil
1 in. (2.5 cm) length *daikon* radish, grated (about 2 Tbsp)
Soy sauce for grated daikon

1. Lay a sheet of aluminum foil (about 12 in. / 30 cm square) on a flat working surface such as a cutting board and poke tiny holes here and there in the foil with a toothpick. Set aside.

2. Beat the eggs vigorously in a bowl and add the chicken broth, water and soy sauce. Heat the vegetable oil in a frying pan over medium-low heat and pour in the egg mixture. As soon as the eggs start to set, begin to stir slowly and constantly with a rubber spatula or a wooden spoon. Cook until fully set but still moist.

3. Spread the eggs in the center of the aluminum foil and wrap the foil around them securely. Press lightly to form a cylinder and allow to cool to room temperature.

4. When cool, unwrap, cut the roll into pieces 1 in. (2.5 cm) thick, and arrange on a serving plate. Mound the grated *daikon* radish on the side and drizzle a little soy sauce on the daikon. Serve at room temperature.

巻き卵

2人分
卵　3個
チキンスープ　小さじ2
水　大さじ3
醤油　小さじ2
植物油　大さじ1
大根おろし　大さじ2
大根おろし用の醤油　適量

1. 平らな場所に、30cmの正方形に切ったアルミホイルを広げる。ところどころ、楊枝などを使って小さな穴をあける。

2. ボウルに卵を入れてよくかき混ぜ、チキンスープ、水、醤油を加える。フライパンを弱火から中火に熱して油をなじませ、卵液を流し込む。固まりそうになったらへらなどでやさしくかき混ぜ、全体が固すぎず、火が通るまで焼く。

3. ホイルの中央に卵を広げ、しっかりと巻く。ホイルを軽く押しながら筒形に整える。室温になるまで冷ます。

4. 冷めたらホイルをはずし、2.5cmに切って皿に盛る。醤油をかけた大根おろしを添える。卵は室温のままでよい。

GRILLED EGGPLANT IN SAUCE

If possible, select smaller, sweeter eggplants
(often sold as "Italian eggplants") for this dish.

Turn the eggplants constantly over a flame until they are charred.

引っくり返しながら、真っ黒になるまでなすを焼く。

Shock in ice water for few seconds to stop cooking.

氷水に数秒とり、加熱を止める。

Gently peel off the blackened skins. You can use a paper towel to peel.

黒くなった皮をむく。キッチンペーパーを使ってもよい。

INGREDIENTS   Serves Two

4 small eggplants
Sauce:
- 2 Tbsp soy sauce
- 1 Tbsp sugar
- 2 tsp chicken broth
- 2 Tbsp water

1 small knob ginger, peeled and grated
2 pinches dried bonito flakes (optional)

1 Fill a large bowl with ice water. Lightly poke holes in the eggplants with a fork. Spear each eggplant on a long fork and grill directly over a gas flame until the entire surface is scorched. Plunge the eggplants in the ice water for a few seconds, then take them out and peel them, leaving the hard stem attached.

2 Mix the sauce ingredients in a small bowl.

3 Arrange the eggplants on a serving plate and pour the sauce over. Serve at room temperature, topped with grated ginger and bonito flakes, if desired.

焼きなすの煮びたし

2人分
なす 小4個
［漬け汁］
- 醤油 大さじ2
- 砂糖 大さじ1
- チキンスープ 小さじ2
- 水 大さじ2

おろししょうが 1片分
かつおぶし（好みで） 2つまみ

1 大きめのボウルに氷水を入れておく。フォークで、なすにところどころ小さな穴をあける。長いフォークを刺し、直火でなすの表面が真っ黒になるまで焼く。氷水に数秒とり、皮をむく。へたは付けたままにしておく。

2 漬け汁の調味料を合わせる。

3 なすを器に盛り、漬け汁をかける。室温になるまで冷まし、おろししょうがと好みでかつおぶしをのせる。

Oil	Oil temperature is critical in frying. For best results read this basic guide to check that your oil is heated to the correct temperature.
油	揚げものは、油の温度が大切です。基本的な温度の見分け方のご参考にしてください。

OIL TEMPERATURE

The secret to crisp, non-greasy fried food is to fill the pan generously with oil—to a depth of about 5cm—and cook the food quickly. Heat the oil to a low (150-160ºC), medium (170-180ºC) or high (around 190ºC) temperature depending on the type of food to be fried. To ascertain the temperature of your oil, drop in a little tempura batter. If the oil is not hot enough for cooking, the batter will sink to the bottom of the pan and stay there. If it sinks to the bottom then rapidly rises, the oil is in the low temperature range; to about halfway down before rising, medium. If the oil has reached a high temperature, the batter will disperse on the surface without sinking at all.

Generally speaking a low oil temperature is suitable for shiso leaves and vegetables such as potatoes; a medium temperature for the likes of kakiage tempura and Japanese pork cutlets, and a high temperature for seafood tempura. Seafood becomes tough when overcooked, so is best fried quickly in oil heated to 180-190ºC. To prevent burning, take care never to heat oil above 190ºC. Place cooked food on a wire rack to drain any excess oil before serving.

油の温度

揚げものをからっと仕上げるには、鍋に油を5cmほどたっぷり入れてなるべく短時間で調理するのがコツです。油の温度は低温（150～160℃）、中温（170～180℃）、高温（190℃前後）とあり、揚げる食材によって使い分けます。温度を見分けるためには、衣を少しだけ油に落としてみましょう。温度が低すぎると、衣は沈んだまま浮かんできません。衣が鍋の底まで沈んですぐ浮かびあがってきたら低温、中ほどまで沈んですぐ浮かびあがってきたら中温です。高温だと、衣は沈まないで油の表面で散ります。

一般的に、低温は青じそやじゃがいもなどの野菜、中温はかき揚げやとんかつ、高温は魚介類の天ぷらに向いています。魚介類は長時間揚げると固くなるので、180～190℃に熱した油で短時間で揚げるとよいでしょう。あまり高温になると焦げてしまいますので、190℃より熱しすぎないよう気を付けます。

揚げた後は網などにのせ、余分な油をきっておきましょう。

Chapter 3
Deep-Fried Dishes
揚げもの 【*Agemono*】

Deep-frying cooks food quickly from all sides, almost like high-temperature steaming, maximizing sweetness and savor. When deep-frying at home, try to work in small batches. Chose a medium-sized (3 to 4 quart / liter) pot and use enough oil to fill the pan 2 in. (5 cm) deep. Transferring fried foods onto a wire rack to drain oil and release steam makes them crispier and healthier.

素材の味を最大限に引き出すため、短時間で調理するのが揚げもののコツです。
家で作るときには、3〜4*l*の鍋に油を5cmほどたっぷり入れます。
揚げたあとは網の上で油をきると、カリッと仕上がり、健康的でもあります。

SHRIMP TEMPURA

It's easy to make great shrimp tempura at home. For frying the tempura, the oil should be at least 2 in. (5 cm) deep.

Cut off the spike above the tail (if attached) to keep the hot oil from spattering when deep-frying.

揚げるときにはねないよう、尾先の端を斜めに切り落とす。

Dusting the shrimp with flour allows the batter to cling more easily.

小麦粉をまぶすことで衣がはがれにくくなる。

When deep-frying, slip the shrimp into the oil headfirst.

海老の頭を下にして揚げる。

- Vegetable tempura (bell peppers, *kabocha*, onion, lotus root, etc.) is made in the same fashion as shrimp—by dusting ingredients with flour, dipping in cold batter, and deep-frying. Vegetables should be sliced about 1/2 in. thick. If frying *shiso* or basil leaves, batter only one side and fry at a lower temperature—about 320°F (160°C).

ピーマン、カボチャ、たまねぎ、れんこんなど野菜の天ぷらも小麦粉をまぶし、冷やした衣を付けて揚げます。野菜は約1cmの厚さに切ります。青じそやバジルは、片面にだけ衣を付け、低めの約160℃の油で揚げます。

INGREDIENTS

Serves Two

Tempura batter:
- 1 egg
- 3/4 cup (180 ml) cold water
- 1 cup (125 g) flour

6 uncooked shrimp, thawed and patted dry if frozen
1/2 cup (60 g) flour for dusting shrimp
Vegetable oil for deep-frying
Set aside 1/2 tsp salt for each serving, or use tempura dipping sauce (see page 58)

1 Beat the egg in a medium bowl and add the cold water and 1 cup flour. Lightly stir with a whisk or chopsticks until almost combined, but with some lumps remaining. Cover the bowl with plastic wrap and refrigerate.

2 Remove the shells from the shrimp but leave the tails attached. Cut off the stiff spike at the tail, if attached. Devein the shrimp. Make a few shallow cuts in the belly side, cutting halfway through the shrimp at 1/2 in. (1 cm) intervals, to prevent them from curling up while frying.

3 Begin heating the vegetable oil to 355º F (180º C) in a medium-sized heavy pot.

4 Dust the shrimp with flour and pat off any excess. Remove the chilled batter from the refrigerator. Holding the shrimp by its tail, dip it into the batter, then slip it into the oil headfirst and deep-fry for 2 minutes until the batter is crisp. Transfer onto a wire rack.

2 Arrange the shrimp on a platter, preferably on absorbent paper to maintain crispness. Mound 1/2 tsp salt on individual serving dishes, or serve with tempura dipping sauce in individual bowls.

海老の天ぷら

2人分

[衣]
- 卵　1個
- 冷水　3/4カップ
- 小麦粉　1カップ

海老　6尾（冷凍の場合は解凍して水気をふく）
小麦粉　1/2カップ
植物油（揚げ油）　適量
塩　各小さじ1/2　または天つゆ
　（p.58を参照）

1 ボウルに卵を入れてかき混ぜる。冷水と小麦粉を加え、泡立て器か菜箸で小麦粉のダマが少し残る程度になるまで混ぜる。ラップをして冷蔵庫で休ませる。

2 海老は尾を残して殻をむく。尾先の端を斜めに切り落とす。背わたを取り、揚げるときに曲がらないよう腹側に1cmごとに浅く切り込みを入れる。

3 揚げ油を180℃に熱する。

4 海老に小麦粉をまぶし、余分な粉ははたいて落とす。冷やしておいた衣を付ける。頭を下にして油に入れ、衣がカリッとするまで2分ほど揚げる。網にのせて油をきる。

5 天ぷらを器に盛る。吸水性のある紙を敷くと、べたつかない。個別に塩または天つゆを添える。

KAKIAGE TEMPURA

The vegetables in *kakiage* are deep-fried in one piece to create a combination of flavors.

INGREDIENTS

Serves Two

1 oz. (30 g) carrot
1 oz. (30 g) *kabocha* squash, or other winter squash
1 oz. (30 g) burdock root or parsnip
4 sprigs chervil, cut into 2 in. (5 cm) lengths
Tempura batter:
- 3 Tbsp flour
- 2 Tbsp cold water

Vegetable oil for deep-frying
Tempura dipping sauce (see page 58)

1. Peel the carrot and squash and cut into thin sticks about 2 in. (5 cm) long. Wash the burdock root in water with a stiff brush, and shred with a vegetable peeler.
2. Begin heating the vegetable oil to 355 °F (180 °C) in a medium-sized heavy pot.
3. Place the carrot, squash, burdock root, chervil, flour and water in a bowl and lightly mix to bind the vegetables together. The batter should be rather runny with some lumps remaining. Place half of the vegetable-batter mixture on a flat spatula and slowly slip it into the oil near the side of the pot, rather than the middle. Deep-fry for 2 minutes, until the batter is crisp. Transfer onto a wire rack. Repeat with remaining mixture.
4. Serve with tempura dipping sauce.

The shredded vegetables tend to scatter in the oil. To bind them together neatly, use a flat spatula such as a turner or fish spatula.

野菜のかき揚げ

2人分

にんじん　30g
かぼちゃ（または同様のスカッシュ）　30g
ごぼう（またはパースニップ）　30g
チャービル（5cmに切る）　4本
［衣］
- 小麦粉　大さじ3
- 冷水　大さじ2

植物油（揚げ油）　適量
天つゆ（p.58を参照）

1. にんじんとかぼちゃは皮をむき、5cmの細い棒状に切る。ごぼうは水の中でたわしなどを使って皮をこそげ、ささがきにする。
2. 揚げ油を180℃に熱する。
3. ボウルに野菜と衣を入れて軽く混ぜる。衣はダマが少し残る程度にゆるく溶いておく。平たいへらに1/2の量をのせ、鍋の側面近くの油に静かにすべらせながら入れる。衣がカリッとするまで2分ほど揚げ、網にのせて油をきる。残りも同様に揚げる。
4. 器にかき揚げを盛り、個別に天つゆを添える。

野菜が広がりやすいので、油に入れたら、へらなどで丸く形を整える。

DEEP-FRIED OYSTERS

Fried oysters are delicious with Worcestershire sauce or with homemade *wasabi*-mayo sauce—it depends on your personal preference.

INGREDIENTS

Serves Two

10 fresh oysters, shelled

1 qt. (1 L) salt water (combine 1 qt. / 1 L cold water with 2 Tbsp salt)

Salt to taste

Ground black pepper to taste

$1/4$ cup (30 g) flour

2 eggs, beaten

1 cup (45 g) *panko* or other bread crumbs

Vegetable oil for deep-frying

Worcestershire sauce or *wasabi*-mayo sauce (see page 24)

2 leaves green-leaf lettuce

2 lemon wedges

1 Rinse the oysters well in the salt water, drain, and pat dry. Sprinkle with salt and black pepper. Place flour, beaten egg, and panko bread crumbs in separate bowls. Dust the oysters with flour and shake off any excess, then dip them in the beaten egg and coat evenly. Roll the oysters in bread crumbs and coat thoroughly, pressing the bread crumbs in by hand.

2 Heat the vegetable oil to 355 °F (180 °C) in a medium-sized heavy pot. Deep-fry the oysters for 3 to 4 minutes until the bread crumbs are golden brown.

3 Arrange the lettuce on a serving plate and top with the oysters and lemon wedges. Drizzle with Worcestershire sauce or serve with wasabi-mayo sauce.

かきフライ

2人分

かき（殻をむいたもの）　10個
塩、黒こしょう（下味用）　適量
小麦粉　$1/4$カップ
溶き卵　2個分
パン粉（またはパンを細かく砕いたもの）　1カップ
植物油（揚げ油）　適量
ウスターソースまたはわさびマヨネーズ（p.24を参照）
レタス　2枚
レモン（櫛形に切る）　2個

1 かきは塩水（冷水1ℓに対して塩大さじ2）でよく洗って水気をふく。塩と黒こしょうをふる。小麦粉、溶き卵、パン粉を別々のボウルに入れておく。かきに小麦粉をつけて余分な粉をはたき落とし、卵、パン粉の順に付けて手で軽く握って形を整える。

2 揚げ油を180℃に熱する。表面が黄金色になるまで、3～4分ほど揚げる。

3 器にレタスを敷いてかきとレモンをのせる。ウスターソースまたはわさびマヨネーズを添える。

JAPANESE PORK CUTLETS

In this dish, Japanese pork cutlets, about ½ in. (1¼ cm) thick, are deep-fried with coarse *panko* bread crumbs. Many supermarkets have started to sell *panko*, but if you can't find it, any white bread crumbs can be used.

INGREDIENTS	Serves Two

2 boneless pork chops, about 4 oz. (120 g) each
Salt to taste
Ground black pepper to taste
¼ cup (30 g) flour
2 eggs, beaten
1 cup (45 g) *panko* or other bread crumbs
Vegetable oil for deep-frying
Worcestershire sauce or soy-sesame sauce (see page 24)
Vegetable garnishes (see below)

1. Season the pork chops on both sides with salt and pepper. Place flour, beaten egg, and bread crumbs in separate bowls. Dust the pork chops with flour, then dip in the beaten egg and coat evenly. Roll in bread crumbs and coat thoroughly, pressing the bread crumbs into the pork chops by hand.

2. Heat the vegetable oil to 355 °F (180 °C) in a medium-sized heavy pot. Deep-fry the pork chops until the bread crumbs turn golden brown. Transfer to a wire rack.

3. Cut the cutlets into 1 in. (2.5 cm) thick slices. Arrange the cutlets on a serving plate along with the vegetable garnishes. Drizzle with Worcestershire sauce or soy-sesame sauce.

● Pork cutlets go well with any vegetable. Shredded cabbage is the classic accompaniment, but I use pieces of carrot and *kabocha* squash cooked in the microwave for 2 to 3 minutes and arranged on the side with parsley.

とんかつ

2人分
豚肉　2枚（各120g）
塩、黒こしょう（下味用）　適量
小麦粉　1/4カップ
溶き卵　2個分
パン粉　1カップ
植物油（揚げ油）　適量
ウスターソースまたは
　ごまだれ（p.24を参照）
付け合わせの野菜（下記参照）

1. 豚肉の両面に塩と黒こしょうをふる。小麦粉を付けて余分な粉をはたき落とし、卵、パン粉の順に付ける。パン粉がはがれないよう、手で軽く肉を押さえる。

2. 揚げ油を180℃に熱する。表面が黄金色になるまで揚げ、網にのせて油をきる。

3. かつを2.5cmに切り、付け合わせの野菜とともに盛る。ウスターソースまたはごまだれを添える。

とんかつは、どんな野菜とも合います。千切りのキャベツが定番ですが、私は小さく切って電子レンジで2～3分蒸したにんじんやかぼちゃを、パセリとともに添えます。

DEEP-FRIED MARINATED CHICKEN BREAST

Chicken breast often turns out dry when cooked, but marinating it in *sake*, soy sauce, and ginger keeps it moist and flavorful.

INGREDIENTS

Serves Two

11 oz. (310 g) chicken breast, cut into bite-sized pieces
1 egg yolk
1 Tbsp soy sauce
2 tsp *sake*
2 tsp grated ginger
2 Tbsp flour
Vegetable oil for deep-frying
½ cup (60 g) cornstarch
2 lemon wedges

1. Beat the egg yolk in a medium bowl, add the soy sauce, sake, grated ginger and flour, and mix until just combined. Coat the chicken and leave for 20 minutes.

2. Heat the vegetable oil to 355 °F (180 °C) in a medium-sized heavy pot. Dust the chicken in the cornstarch and shake off any excess. Deep-fry the chicken in the oil until the coating becomes crisp, 5 to 6 minutes. Transfer onto a wire rack.

3. Arrange on a serving platter, preferably on absorbent paper, and put the lemon wedges on the side.

鶏のから揚げ

2人分

鶏胸肉（一口大に切る）　310g
卵黄　1個
醤油　大さじ1
酒　小さじ2
おろししょうが　小さじ2
小麦粉　大さじ2
植物油（揚げ油）　適量
コーンスターチ　½カップ
レモン（櫛形）　2個

1. ボウルに卵黄を入れてかき混ぜる。醤油、酒、おろししょうが、小麦粉を加えて全体がなじむまで混ぜる。鶏肉にからめて20分おく。

2. 揚げ油を180℃に熱する。鶏肉にコーンスターチをまぶして余分な粉をはたき落とす。表面がカリッとするまで5〜6分揚げる。網にのせて油をきる。

3. 器に盛り（できれば吸水性の紙を敷く）、レモンを添える。

DEEP-FRIED COD

A comforting yet appetizing dish full of fragrance, with soy sauce, lemon peel, and parsley.

INGREDIENTS Serves Two

3 1/2 oz. (200 g) cod fillets
2 Tbsp soy sauce
1 Tbsp *sake*
Salad:
  { 2 tender leaves green-leaf lettuce, washed and dried
  1/2 small red bell pepper, seeded and thinly sliced
  1/2 small yellow bell pepper, seeded and thinly sliced
Vegetable oil for deep-frying
1/2 cup (60 g) cornstarch
1 tsp lemon peel, minced
1 tsp parsley leaves, minced

1 Remove the skin and pin bones from the cod and cut into large pieces. Combine the soy sauce and sake in a bowl, coat the cod thoroughly, and leave for 15 minutes.

2 To make the salad, tear the lettuce into pieces. Combine the lettuce and bell peppers and refrigerate.

3 Heat the vegetable oil to 355 °F (180 °C) in a medium-sized heavy pot. Add the cornstarch, lemon peel, and parsley leaves directly to the bowl in which the cod is marinating and mix to coat the cod thoroughly. Deep-fry in the oil until the batter is lightly browned, 3 to 4 minutes. Transfer onto a wire rack. Arrange the salad in a serving bowl and serve the cod on top.

たらのから揚げ

2人分
たらの切り身　200 g
醤油　大さじ2
酒　大さじ1
［サラダ］
　{ レタス　2枚
　　ピーマン（赤、黄）　各小1/2個
植物油（揚げ油）　適量
コーンスターチ　1/2カップ
レモンの皮（細かいみじん切り）
　小さじ1
パセリ（細かいみじん切り）
　小さじ1

1 たらは皮と骨をのぞき、食べやすく切る。ボウルに醤油と酒を入れて混ぜ、たらを漬けて15分おく。

2 レタスをちぎり、薄切りにした赤、黄ピーマンと合わせて冷蔵庫に入れておく。

3 揚げ油を180℃に熱する。たらを漬けたボウルにコーンスターチ、レモンの皮、パセリを入れ、全体を混ぜてなじませる。表面が薄茶色になるまで3〜4分揚げる。網にのせて油をきる。器にサラダを敷き、たらをのせる。

DEEP-FRIED TOFU

This is another great tofu dish. Mixing the grated radish, ginger, and scallions into the broth makes a refreshing sauce that lightens the fried tofu.

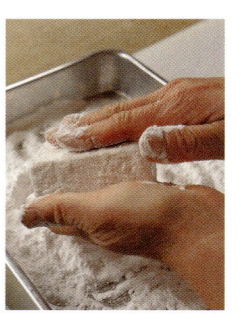

Pat off any excess cornstarch from the tofu.

余分なコーンスターチをはたいて落とす。

Tofu can be deep-fried by submerging it halfway in the oil in a heavy-duty frying pan.

鉄フライパンに油を豆腐が半分つかるぐらいまで入れ、片側ずつ揚げてもよい。

INGREDIENTS

Serves Two

Broth:
- 1 Tbsp chicken broth
- 4 Tbsp water
- 2 tsp soy sauce
- 2 tsp sugar

½ block firm tofu (about 6 oz. / 170 g), cut in two

1 Tbsp cornstarch

Vegetable oil for deep-frying

1 in. (2.5 cm) length *daikon* radish, grated (about 2 Tbsp total)

½ tsp ground or crushed chili pepper

1 large knob ginger, peeled and grated

1 scallion, chopped

1 Combine the chicken broth, water, soy sauce and sugar in a small saucepan and heat to dissolve the sugar. Set aside. Begin heating the vegetable oil to 355 °F (180 °C) in a medium-sized heavy pot.

2 Dust the tofu with cornstarch, brushing off any excess. Place a piece of tofu on a wire skimmer or slotted spoon and plunge in the oil. Deep-fry until the surface becomes golden brown, about 6 minutes, and transfer onto a wire rack. Repeat with the other piece of tofu.

3 Place the fried tofu in a serving bowl and pour in the broth. Mix the grated daikon radish and ground chili pepper together and mound on the tofu, followed by the grated ginger and chopped scallion. Just before eating, mix the grated daikon, ginger and scallions into the broth.

揚げだし豆腐

2人分

[だし汁]
- チキンスープ 大さじ1
- 水 大さじ4
- 醤油 小さじ2
- 砂糖 小さじ2

豆腐（木綿） ½丁（170g）

コーンスターチ 大さじ1

植物油（揚げ油） 適量

大根おろし 大さじ2

唐辛子（粉またはみじん切り） 小さじ½

おろししょうが 1片分

細ねぎ（みじん切り） 1本分

1 小鍋にだし汁の材料を入れ、砂糖が溶けるまで温める。揚げ油を180℃に熱する。

2 豆腐を半分に切り、コーンスターチをまぶして余分な粉をはたき落とす。網じゃくしや穴のあいたお玉に豆腐をのせて油に沈める。表面が黄金色になるまで6分ほど揚げ、網にのせて油をきる。もう半分の豆腐も同様に揚げる。

3 器に豆腐を入れ、だし汁をかける。大根おろしと唐辛子を混ぜたもの、おろししょうが、細ねぎを豆腐にのせる。食べる直前にそれらをだし汁に混ぜる。

CHICKEN WINGS ESCABECHE

Marinating the chicken wings after frying makes them light and refreshing. You can keep the wings refrigerated in the marinade for up to 3 days.

INGREDIENTS

Serves Two

6 large chicken wings
½ cup (60 g) flour
Marinade:
- ½ cup (120 ml) white or red wine vinegar
- ⅓ cup (80 ml) chicken broth
- 1 ⅓ cup (320 ml) water
- 3 Tbsp soy sauce
- 3 Tbsp sugar
- ½ tsp crushed chili pepper

Vegetable oil for deep-frying
½ onion, peeled and shredded
¼ carrot, peeled and shredded
1 tsp minced lemon peel
2 scallions, chopped
2 tsp toasted sesame seeds

1 Heat the vegetable oil to 355 °F (180 °C) in a medium-sized heavy pot. Dust the chicken with the flour and deep-fry in the oil until the surface is golden brown, about 5 to 6 minutes. Transfer onto a wire rack.

2 Combine all marinade ingredients in a saucepan and bring to a simmer. Add the fried chicken wings, onion, and carrot, stir once and turn off the heat. Allow to cool to room temperature.

3 Arrange the chicken in a shallow serving bowl and top with the onion and carrot. Sprinkle with the lemon peel, scallions, and sesame seeds.

鶏の南蛮漬け

2人分

鶏の手羽先　6本
小麦粉　½カップ
［マリネ液］
- 白または赤ワインビネガー
　½カップ
- チキンスープ　⅓カップ
- 水　1⅓カップ
- 醤油　大さじ3
- 砂糖　大さじ3
- 唐辛子（みじん切り）
　小さじ½

植物油（揚げ油）　適量
たまねぎ（薄切り）　½個
にんじん（薄切り）　¼本
レモンの皮（細かいみじん切り）
　小さじ1
細ねぎ（みじん切り）　2本分
いりごま　小さじ2

1 揚げ油を180℃に熱する。鶏肉に小麦粉をまぶし、表面が黄金色になるまで5〜6分揚げる。網にのせて油をきる。

2 マリネ液の材料を小鍋に入れて煮立てる。鶏肉、たまねぎ、にんじんを加え、さっと混ぜて火を止める。室温になるまで冷ます。

3 浅めの器に鶏肉をのせ、たまねぎとにんじんを盛る。レモンの皮、細ねぎ、いりごまを散らす。

Sauces 2 / たれ2

Here's how to make the tsuyu dipping sauce for the tempura on pp. 42 and 44. Dip in salt or sauce according to preference.

p.42、44の天ぷらに添えるつゆの作り方です。塩か天つゆに、お好みで付けていただきます。

TEMPURA DIPPING SAUCE

The grated *daikon* radish and ginger cut through the oiliness of tempura and aid in digestion.

INGREDIENTS makes about 1 cup (240 ml)

2 Tbsp chicken broth
1/2 cup (120 ml) water
2 Tbsp soy sauce
1 Tbsp sugar
1 Tbsp grated *daikon* radish per serving
1 tsp grated ginger per serving

Combine all dipping sauce ingredients, except the daikon and ginger, in a small saucepan. Bring to a simmer, wait for 30 seconds, and remove from heat. Cool to room temperature. Pour into small individual serving bowls, place a mound of grated daikon radish in the sauce, and top with a little grated ginger. Just before eating, mix the grated *daikon* radish and ginger into the sauce.

天つゆ

おろした大根やしょうがは、揚げものの消化を助けます。

できあがり 1カップ

チキンスープ　大さじ2
水　1/2カップ
醤油　大さじ2
砂糖　大さじ1
大根おろし　各大さじ1
おろししょうが　各小さじ1

大根おろし、おろししょうが以外の材料を小鍋に入れて煮立てる。煮立って30秒したら火からはずし、室温になるまで冷ます。それぞれの器につゆを注ぐ。大根おろしを入れ、その上におろししょうがを少しのせる。食べる直前に、大根としょうがをつゆに混ぜる。

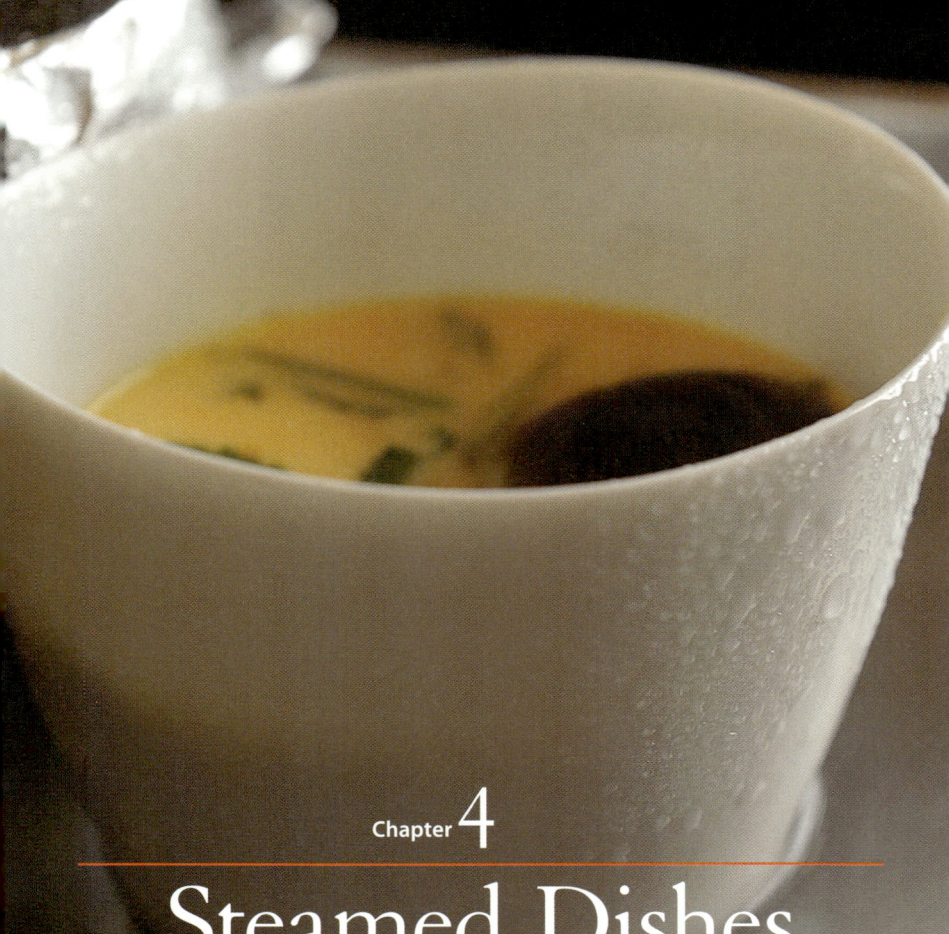

Chapter 4
Steamed Dishes
蒸しもの【*Mushimono*】

Steaming cooks foods gently and evenly—the perfect method
for delicate fish, eggs, and vegetables.
You don't need a steamer to make these dishes;
you can use the stovetop, the oven, or even the microwave.

ゆっくりとむらなく火が通る蒸しものは、魚、卵、野菜など
繊細な食材の調理にぴったりです。
せいろがなくても、料理用ストーブ、オーブン、電子レンジで蒸すことができます。

SAKE-STEAMED CLAMS

Steaming in *sake* is the best way to enjoy the delicate sweetness of fresh clams.

INGREDIENTS

Serves Two

14 oz. (400 g) clams or unshelled steamer clams
1 qt. (1 L) water
2 Tbsp salt
½ cup (120 ml) *sake*
½ cup (120 ml) water
1 tsp soy sauce
Juice squeezed from 2 large knobs peeled, grated ginger (about 2 tsp)
1 to 2 scallions, chopped

1 Rinse the clams in running cold water and place in a bowl. Mix the 1 qt. (1 L) water and 2 Tbsp salt and pour over the clams to barely cover. Cover and let stand for 20 minutes so that the clams expel all their sand, then rinse the clams in cold water.

2 Place the clams, sake, ½ cup water, and soy sauce in a single layer in a pan and bring to a simmer. Cover with a lid and cook the clams until they open, for 5 to 10 minutes. Discard any unopened clams.

3 Arrange the clams and cooking liquid in a serving bowl and sprinkle with the ginger juice and chopped scallions.

あさりの酒蒸し

2人分
あさり　400g
酒　½カップ
水　½カップ
醤油　小さじ1
しょうがの絞り汁　約小さじ2
細ねぎ（みじん切り）　1〜2本分

1 あさりは流水で洗ってボウルに入れる。ほとんどかぶるぐらいの塩水（水1ℓに対して塩大さじ2）に漬け、20分おいて砂抜きをする。流水ですすぐ。

2 重ならないように鍋にあさりを入れ、酒、水、醤油を加えて煮立てる。ふたをしてあさりが開くまで5〜10分蒸す。開かないあさりは取り除く。

3 器に、あさりを汁ごと盛る。しょうがの絞り汁をかけ、細ねぎを散らす。

STEAMED VEGETABLES WITH PEANUT BUTTER DRESSING

For this dish the vegetables are steamed in the microwave, a great method for retaining flavor and nutrients.

INGREDIENTS

Serves Two

Peanut butter dressing:
- 3 Tbsp salted peanut butter
- 3 Tbsp soy sauce
- 1 1/2 Tbsp white wine vinegar
- 1 1/2 Tbsp sugar
- 1 Tbsp crushed peanuts

1 medium all-purpose potato, peeled
1/2 medium carrot, peeled
3 1/2 oz. (100 g) *kabocha* squash or other winter squash
10 green beans, trimmed and cut into 2 in. (5 cm) lengths
3 Tbsp water

1 Combine all peanut butter dressing ingredients in a small bowl.

2 Cut the potato, carrot, and squash into thin sticks, 2 in. (5 cm) long. Place the vegetables in a heat-proof bowl and sprinkle with the water. Cover with plastic wrap and microwave until tender, about 2 minutes. Unwrap and drain on paper towels or in a sieve.

3 Arrange the vegetables in a serving bowl with extra dressing on the side.

- Zucchini, asparagus, broccoli, and cauliflower are also good for steaming.

蒸し野菜の
ピーナツバターだれ

2人分

[ピーナツバターだれ]
- ピーナツバター（有塩） 大さじ3
- 醤油 大さじ3
- 白ワインビネガー 大さじ1 1/2
- 砂糖 大さじ1 1/2
- ピーナツ（砕いたもの） 大さじ1

じゃがいも 1個
にんじん 1/2本
かぼちゃ（または同様のスカッシュ） 100g
いんげん（筋を取って5cmに切る） 10本
水 大さじ3

1 ピーナツバターだれの材料をすべて混ぜ、器に入れる。

2 じゃがいも、にんじん、かぼちゃは5cmの細い棒状に切る。耐熱ボウルに野菜を入れ、水をふる。ラップをして、やわらかくなるまで電子レンジに2分ほどかける。キッチンペーパーかざるに置いて水気をきる。

3 器に野菜を盛り、ピーナツバターだれを適量かける。残りのたれは添える。

ズッキーニ、アスパラガス、ブロッコリー、カリフラワーなども蒸し野菜に合います。

STEAMED EGG CUSTARD

As the eggs set into a savory custard, they absorb and hold the succulent juices from the chicken, *shiitake* mushrooms, and shrimp. Serve as a hot appetizer.

Strain the egg mixture through a fine-mesh sieve.

目の細かいざるで卵液をこす。

Oven-steaming is simple and easy if you have a pan with a high rim.

ふちの高い器があれば、オーブンで手軽に蒸しものを作ることができる。

- To check doneness, remove a cup from the oven, unwrap, and use a bamboo skewer or toothpick to poke a hole in the custard all the way to the bottom of the cup. If clear liquid wells up out of the hole, the custard is done. If the liquid is cloudy, return to the oven for another 5 minutes, then check again.

  卵液が固まったか確かめるには、オーブンから器を出し、竹串かようじを底まで刺してみます。澄んだ汁が出たら蒸しあがり。汁がにごっているようならオーブンに戻し、さらに5分蒸し焼きにしてから再確認します。

INGREDIENTS   Serves Two

Two oven-proof cups or small bowls, each able to hold
  1 cup (16 oz. / 240 ml) liquid
An oven-proof pan with a rim about 1 1/2 in. (3 to 4 cm) high,
  large enough to hold both custard cups
Egg mixture:
- 2 large eggs
- 1/3 cup (80 ml) chicken broth
- 1 1/3 cups (320 ml) water
- 2 tsp soy sauce

2 fresh *shiitake* mushrooms, cleaned and stems trimmed
2 medium shrimp, shelled and deveined
1 1/2 oz. (40 to 50 g) chicken breast, without skin, halved
Leaves from 2 sprigs chervil or *mitsuba* herb
Slivered lemon peel
Hot water
2 pinches ground chili pepper

1 Preheat the oven to 355 °F (180 °C).

2 Crack the eggs into a bowl and mix gently so as not to create bubbles. Add the chicken broth, water, and soy sauce, and strain through a fine-mesh sieve to make a smooth mixture.

3 Divide the mushrooms, shrimp, chicken, and chervil leaves between the cups and pour equal amounts of egg mixture into each. Top with lemon peel and cover each cup with foil. Put the cups in a pan with a high rim and add enough hot water to come 1/2 in. (1 cm) up the sides of the cups. Transfer the pan to the oven and bake for 30 minutes. When done (see sidebar) remove from the oven and allow to cool slightly.

4 When cool enough to handle, unwrap and serve. Top with ground chili pepper if desired.

茶碗蒸し

2人分

耐熱の容器（1カップの卵液を入れられるもの）　2つ
耐熱の器（2つの容器が入り、3〜4cmの高さがあるもの）　1つ
［卵液］
- 卵　2個
- チキンスープ　1/3カップ
- 水　1 1/3カップ
- 醤油　小さじ2

しいたけ（軸を除き、汚れをふく）　2枚
海老（殻をむき、背わたを取る）　2尾
鶏胸肉（皮なし。半分に切る）　40〜50g
チャービル（またはみつば）　2本
レモンの皮　適量
熱湯
粉唐辛子　2つまみ

1　オーブンを180℃に温めておく。

2　卵をボウルに入れ、泡ができないよう静かにかき混ぜる。チキンスープ、水、醤油を加え、目の細かいざるでこす。

3　しいたけ、海老、鶏肉、チャービルを2つの容器に同量ずつ入れ、卵液を注ぐ。レモンの皮をのせ、アルミホイルをかぶせて耐熱の器に置き、器の底から1cmまで熱湯を注ぐ。器ごとオーブンに入れて30分蒸し焼きにする（左ページ参照）。蒸しあがったら出し、少し冷ます。

4　器を持てるほど冷めたらホイルをはずす。好みで、粉唐辛子をふる。

STEAMED SALMON WITH TOFU AND MUSHROOMS

The *kombu* need not be eaten—it may be a bit tough—but its *umami* surely enhances this dish.

INGREDIENTS

Serves Two

- 2 pieces dried kombu kelp, each about 2 in. (5 cm) square
- 2/3 cup (160 ml) *sake*
- 2/3 cup (160 ml) water
- 1 1/2 Tbsp soy sauce
- 2 salmon fillets or steaks, about 4 oz. (120 g) each
- Salt to taste
- Ground black pepper to taste
- 1/2 block tofu, about 6 oz. (170 g)
- 4 oz. (120 g) mushrooms, such as *shiitake*, *maitake*, *enoki*, or regular button mushrooms
- Juice of 1/2 lemon
- Slivered lemon peel (optional)
- 6 snow peas, trimmed and blanched in boiling water (optional)

1 Combine the *kombu*, sake and water in a bowl and leave overnight. Remove the kombu and add the soy sauce to the liquid.

2 Sprinkle the salmon slices with salt and pepper on both sides. Cut the tofu in half. Wipe the mushrooms clean, trim hard parts off the stems, and cut or tear into bite-sized pieces.

3 Lay a piece of kombu in a heat-proof, shallow bowl suitable for one serving. Place half the mushrooms, tofu and salmon on the kombu and pour in half the sake-soy sauce mixture. Repeat in a separate bowl with the remaining ingredients. Cover each dish with plastic wrap and microwave for 4 to 5 minutes.

4 To serve, unwrap and sprinkle with the lemon juice. Top with the slivered lemon peel and blanched snow peas, if using.

鮭と豆腐の きのこ蒸し

2人分

- 昆布（乾。5cm角）　2枚
- 酒　2/3カップ
- 水　2/3カップ
- 醤油　大さじ1 1/2
- 鮭の切り身　2枚（各120g）
- 塩、黒こしょう（下味用）　適量
- 豆腐　1/2丁（170g）
- しいたけ、まいたけ、えのき、マッシュルームなどのきのこ　120g
- レモン汁　1/2個分
- レモンの皮（細切り。好みで）
- さやえんどう（筋を取り、ゆでておく。好みで）　6枚

1 昆布は酒と水に一晩漬けておく。昆布を取り出し、醤油を加える。

2 鮭は両面に塩と黒こしょうをふって下味をつける。豆腐は半分に切る。きのこは汚れをふいて軸を取り除き、一口大に切る。

3 1人分の浅めの耐熱皿に昆布を1枚敷く。きのこ、豆腐、鮭の半量をのせ、酒と醤油だしの半量を注ぐ。もう1人分も同様に作る。ラップをして、電子レンジに4～5分かける。

4 ラップをはずし、レモン汁をかける。好みで、レモンの皮とさやえんどうをのせる。

Dashi 1
だし 1

Here's how to make *Dashi* indispensable to authentic Japanese cooking. Choose easy dashi or extra-rich dashi to suit your requirements.

本格的な和食を作りたい方のために、2種類のだしをご紹介します。

EASY *DASHI*
INGREDIENTS   makes about 1.8 quarts (1.8 l)

2 pieces dried *kombu* kelp, each about 4 in. (10 cm) square
3 cups (30 g) lightly packed dried bonito flakes
2 qts. (2 L) water

1 Combine the *kombu* and water in a pot over medium-low heat. The water should be approaching a boil after about 20 minutes. Once the water comes to a boil, immediately turn off the heat and remove the kombu with tongs.

2 Add the dried bonito flakes all at once. Wait until they absorb the water and sink.

3 Strain the broth through a fine-mesh sieve. For extra-clear dashi, line the strainer with two layers of cheesecloth.

EXTRA-RICH *DASHI*
INGREDIENTS   makes about 1.8 quarts (1.8 l)

1 oz. (30 g) dried *kombu* kelp
1 3/4 oz. (50 g) dried bonito flakes
2 qts. (2 L) water, preferably soft bottled water

1 Combine the *kombu* and water in a stock pot over high heat. When the water temperature reaches 140 °F (60 °C), lower the heat to maintain a constant water temperature of 140 °F (60 °C). Steep the kombu in the water for 1 hour to extract its full umami flavor. Remove the kombu from the pot.

2 Increase the heat and bring the water temperature up to 185 °F (85 °C). Turn off the heat, add the dried bonito flakes all at once, and wait until all the flakes sink to the bottom of the pot (you can push them into the water with chopsticks or a fork, but do not stir the *dashi* or it will become cloudy and strong-tasting).

3 Line a sieve with the cheese cloth and strain the dashi. Do not squeeze the bonito flakes in the cloth, but let them drain naturally for several minutes until no more dashi passes through the strainer.

簡易だし
できあがり 1.8ℓ

昆布（乾）10cm角　2枚
かつおぶし　3カップ（30g）
水　2ℓ

1 鍋に水と昆布を入れ、弱火から中火にかける。20分ほどかけて沸騰するように火を調整する。沸騰したら火を止め、昆布を取り出す。

2 かつおぶしを一度に入れ、吸水して沈むまでおく。

3 目の細かいざるでだしをこす。より澄んだだしをとるときは、ざるにふきんを二重に敷いてからこす。

本格だし
できあがり 1.8ℓ

昆布（乾）30g
かつおぶし　50g
水（軟水が望ましい）　2ℓ

1 鍋に水と昆布を入れ、強火にかける。温度が60℃になったら火を弱め、温度計を見て60℃を保つように調整する。うま味を十分に引き出すため、昆布を1時間漬けておいてから取り出す。

2 火を強めて85℃にする。85℃になったら火を止め、かつおぶしを一度に入れる。吸水して沈むまでおく（かき混ぜないこと）。

3 ざるにふきんを敷いてだしをこす。無理に絞らず、自然に水気がきれるまで待つ。

Chapter 5
Simmered Dishes
煮もの【*Nimono*】

Simmering meats, fish and vegetables with just enough heat makes them tender and succulent. The dishes in this section are cooked without a lid, but they can be partially covered if the ingredients begin to dry out on top.

ちょうどよい火加減で煮込むだけで、うま味たっぷりのおいしい煮物ができます。レシピではふたを開けたままですが、汁気が飛びすぎるようなら、部分的に覆いをしてもよいでしょう。

BRAISED BEEF AND POTATOES

Beef and potatoes cooked in sweetened soy sauce is a ubiquitous home-cooked dish in Japan that just about everyone loves.

INGREDIENTS

Serves Two

4 oz. (120 g) ground beef
2 large potatoes (waxy type if available, rather than baking type)
1 Tbsp vegetable oil
1/3 cup (45 g) shelled or frozen green peas
1 cup (240 ml) water
2 Tbsp soy sauce
1 Tbsp sugar
2 scallions, thinly sliced

1 Wash the potatoes, peel, and cut into bite-sized pieces.

2 Heat the vegetable oil in a medium-sized saucepan. Add the beef and stir until it changes color. Add the potatoes, water, soy sauce, and sugar, and bring to a simmer over medium-high heat. Lower the heat and simmer uncovered until the potatoes are tender, about 20 minutes. Add the green peas and simmer until the liquid is almost gone.

3 Arrange the beef and potatoes in a serving bowl and top with the sliced scallions.

肉じゃが

2人分

牛ひき肉　120g
じゃがいも　大2個
植物油　大さじ1
グリーンピース　45g
水　1カップ
醤油　大さじ2
砂糖　大さじ1
細ねぎ（小口切り）　2本分

1 じゃがいもは皮をむき、一口大に切る。

2 油を熱し、ひき肉を色が変わるまで炒める。じゃがいも、水、醤油、砂糖を加えて中火から強火で煮立てる。中火にし、ふたをせずにじゃがいもがやわらかくなるまで20分ほど煮る。グリーンピースを入れ、汁気がほとんどなくなるまでさらに煮る。

3 器に盛り、細ねぎを散らす。

SIMMERED NAPA CABBAGE AND PORK SLICES

The meltingly tender texture and sweet flavor of napa cabbage make it a popular vegetable for stews in Japan.

INGREDIENTS   Serves Two

1/2 head napa cabbage, about 2 1/4 lbs. (1 kg)

7 oz. (200 g) sliced fresh pork belly or bacon, cut into 2 in. (5 cm) pieces

1 1/4 cups (300 ml) water

2 Tbsp soy sauce

1 Tbsp sugar

Ground black pepper

Slivered lemon peel (optional)

1 Cut off the base of the cabbage, wash the leaves, and cut them across the grain into 2 in. (5 cm) pieces.

2 Place the water, soy sauce, sugar, and pork belly or bacon in a medium-sized pot and bring to a simmer. Add the cabbage. When the liquid returns to a boil, lower the heat and cook uncovered at a gentle simmer until the cabbage is tender, about 15 minutes.

3 To serve, dust with ground black pepper and top with slivered lemon peel if desired.

● If you can, ask your butcher for fresh pork belly sliced paper-thin. Fresh pork belly makes a clearer-tasting broth than bacon.

豚肉と白菜の煮もの

2人分

白菜　1/2個

豚バラ肉またはベーコン
　　（5cmに切る）　200g

水　1 1/4カップ

醤油　大さじ2

砂糖　大さじ1

黒こしょう　適量

レモンの皮（細切り。好みで）

1 白菜は根元の硬い部分を切り落とし、洗って5cmに切る。

2 鍋に水、醤油、砂糖、豚肉またはベーコンを入れて煮立てる。白菜を加える。ふたをせず、沸騰しないように火加減を見ながら、白菜がやわらかくなるまで15分ほど煮る。

3 器に盛り、黒こしょうをふる。好みで、レモンの皮をのせる。

入手しにくい場合は、豚バラ肉は精肉店で薄く切ってもらいましょう。新鮮な豚バラ肉は、ベーコンよりすっきりした味わいです。

KABOCHA SQUASH AND BACON STEW

Kabocha squash is worth seeking out for its sweet, buttery flavor, but any hard-shell squash can be substituted.

INGREDIENTS

Serves Two

7 oz. (200 g) *kabocha* squash
3 1/2 oz. (100 g) sliced bacon (3 to 4 regular slices), chopped
1 cup (240 ml) water
1 Tbsp soy sauce
1/2 Tbsp sugar
1 to 2 sprigs parsley, chopped

1 If using a whole squash, cut in half and remove the seeds and stringy pulp with a spoon. Cut each half into wedges, then cut into 2 in. (5 cm) pieces until you have about 7 oz. (200 g) total. Use a sharp knife to peel off the dark green rind off in places. Place the squash in a heat-proof dish, cover with plastic wrap, and microwave for 3 minutes.

2 Place the squash, chopped bacon, water, soy sauce, and sugar in a saucepan over medium-high heat and bring to a simmer. Lower the heat and simmer uncovered until the liquid is almost gone, about 10 minutes.

3 Arrange the squash and bacon in a serving bowl and sprinkle with chopped parsley.

If you have any leftovers, this dish tastes even better reheated the next day.

かぼちゃと ベーコンの煮もの

2人分
かぼちゃ　200 g
ベーコンスライス　100 g
水　1カップ
醤油　大さじ1
砂糖　大さじ1/2
パセリ（みじん切り）　1～2本分

1 かぼちゃは種とワタを取って櫛形に切り、さらに5 cm角に切る（この状態で200 g）。皮の硬い部分はそぎ落とす。耐熱皿に入れてラップをし、電子レンジに3分かける。

2 かぼちゃ、細切りにしたベーコン、水、醤油、砂糖を鍋に入れ、中火から強火で煮立てる。火を弱め、汁気がほとんどなくなるまでふたをあけたまま10分ほど煮る。

3 器に盛り、パセリを散らす。

煮物が残ったら、翌日に温め直していただけます。味が染みていっそうおいしくなっているでしょう。

SWEET-AND-SOUR CHICKEN WINGS

The refreshing aroma of vinegar and lemon makes this simmered chicken dish perfect for summer. It's good hot, warm, or cold.

INGREDIENTS

Serves Two

- 6 large chicken wings
- 1 tsp vegetable oil
- ½ cup (120 ml) white wine vinegar
- ½ cup (120 ml) water
- 2 Tbsp soy sauce
- 1 Tbsp sugar
- 6 thinly sliced lemon rounds
- 1 to 2 sprigs parsley, chopped

1 Heat the vegetable oil in a frying pan and sear the chicken on both sides until lightly browned.

2 Place the seared chicken, white wine vinegar, water, soy sauce, and sugar in a medium-sized pot and bring to a simmer. Lower the heat and cook at a gentle simmer until the liquid is reduced but enough remains to cook the lemon slices. Add the lemon and continue to cook until the remaining liquid is almost gone.

3 Place the chicken and lemon in a serving bowl and sprinkle with the chopped parsley.

手羽先の ワインビネガー煮

2人分

- 手羽先 6本
- 植物油 小さじ1
- 白ワインビネガー ½カップ
- 水 ½カップ
- 醤油 大さじ2
- 砂糖 大さじ1
- レモン（薄い輪切り） 6枚
- パセリ（みじん切り） 1～2本分

1 油を熱し、鶏肉の両面が薄茶色になるまで焼く。

2 鶏肉、白ワインビネガー、水、醤油、砂糖を鍋に入れて煮立てる。火を弱め、汁気が減るまで煮る。レモンを入れ、汁気がほとんどなくなるまでさらに煮る。

3 器に鶏肉とレモンを盛り、パセリを散らす。

SIMMERED CALAMARI AND *DAIKON* RADISH

Calamari makes a surprisingly fragrant, deep-flavored broth, which is absorbed beautifully by the *daikon* radish in this dish.

INGREDIENTS　　　　　　　　　　　　　　Serves Two

3 in. (7.5 cm) length *daikon* radish, about 10 oz. (300 g), peeled and cut into bite-sized pieces

4 green beans, tops and tails removed

7 oz. (200 g) calamari, thawed if frozen

1 cup (240 ml) water

1 Tbsp plus 1 tsp soy sauce

1 Tbsp sugar

Pinch crushed chili pepper (or *shichimi* spice powder)

1 Place the daikon radish in a heat-proof dish, cover with plastic wrap, and microwave for 5 minutes. Cut the green beans into 1 in. (2.5 cm) pieces.

2 Place the daikon, calamari, water, soy sauce and sugar in a medium-sized pot and bring to a simmer. Lower the heat and simmer uncovered until 3/4 of the liquid is gone. Add the green beans and cook until they are tender.

3 To serve, sprinkle with crushed chili pepper.

いかと大根の煮もの

2人分

大根（皮をむき、一口大に切る）
　300 g
いんげん（両端を切る）　4本
いか（冷凍の場合は解凍しておく）
　200 g
水　1カップ
醤油　大さじ1と小さじ1
砂糖　大さじ1
唐辛子（みじん切り。または七味
　唐辛子）　適量

1 大根を耐熱容器に入れ、ラップをかけて電子レンジに5分かける。いんげんは2.5 cmに切る。

2 鍋に大根、いか、水、醤油、砂糖を入れて煮立てる。火を弱め、ふたをせずに汁気が1/4になるまで煮る。いんげんを入れ、やわらかくなるまでさらに煮る。

3 器に盛り、七味唐辛子をふる。

GINGER MACKEREL

Blanching fish with a strong taste like mackerel in boiling water removes much of the "fishy" flavor.

INGREDIENTS   Serves Two

2 cups (480 ml) water for blanching mackerel
2 mackerel fillets, preferably skin-on, each about 4 oz. (120 g)
1 knob ginger, peeled and thinly sliced
¾ cup (180 ml) water
¾ cup (180 ml) *sake*
¼ cup (60 ml) soy sauce
2 Tbsp sugar

1 Bring water to a boil in a small saucepan. Have ice water ready in a medium bowl. Blanch one fillet for 10 seconds and immediately plunge it into the ice water. Repeat with the other fillet. Pat the mackerel dry with paper towels.

2 Place the mackerel in a saucepan and add the ¾ cup (180 ml) water, sake, soy sauce, and sugar. Bring to a simmer over medium-high heat. Add the ginger, lower the heat, and cook uncovered at a gentle simmer until the liquid is almost gone, about 10 minutes.

Using a slotted spoon, plunge the mackerel slice in boiling water.
さばを熱湯にくぐらせる。穴あきスプーンにのせるとやりやすい。

Shock the mackerel slice in ice water, then pat dry with paper towels.
氷水で瞬間的に冷やし、ペーパーで、水気をきる。

さばのしょうが煮

2人分
さばの切り身　2切れ（各120g）
しょうが（皮をむき、薄切りにする）
　1片分
水　¾カップ
酒　¾カップ
醤油　¼カップ
砂糖　大さじ2

1 湯（2カップ）をわかす。ボウルに氷水を用意する。さばを10秒湯通しし、すぐに氷水にとる。もう1切れも同様にする。キッチンペーパーで包んで軽く叩き、水気をきる。

2 鍋にさば、水、酒、醤油、砂糖を入れる。中火から強火で煮立てる。しょうがを加えて火を弱め、ふたをせずに汁気がほとんどなくなるまで10分ほど煮る。

KIMPIRA

Kimpira, a classic dish on Japanese home tables, features burdock root and carrot cooked with soy sauce, sugar, and hot chili pepper.

INGREDIENTS

Serves Two

- 9 in. (22 cm) length burdock root, about 3 1/2 oz. (100 g)
- 1/3 medium carrot, peeled and cut into thin sticks
- 1/2 tsp crushed chili pepper or 1/2 dried hot chili pepper sliced into thin rounds
- 2 tsp vegetable oil
- 2 tsp soy sauce
- 1/2 Tbsp sugar
- 1 tsp toasted sesame seeds

1. Scrub the burdock root in cold water with a stiff brush (peeling is not necessary), and use a vegetable peeler to shave it into thin shreds.

2. Heat the vegetable oil in a frying pan or saucepan over medium-high heat, then add the burdock root, carrot, and chili pepper. Cook until the burdock root and carrot shed their juices and become slightly soft. Add the sugar and soy sauce and cook, stirring continuously, until the liquid is almost gone. Take care not to scorch the soy sauce.

3. Sprinkle with the sesame seeds before serving.

きんぴら

2人分

ごぼう　100 g
にんじん（皮をむき、細い棒状に切る）　1/3本
唐辛子（みじん切り。または小口切り）　小さじ1/2
植物油　小さじ2
醤油　小さじ2
砂糖　大さじ1/2
いりごま　小さじ1

1. ごぼうは冷水のなかでたわしでこする（皮をむく必要はない）。皮むき器で薄切りにする。

2. 中火から強火に油を熱し、ごぼう、にんじん、唐辛子を野菜がしんなりするまで炒める。砂糖と醤油を加え、汁気がほとんどなくなるまでさらに炒める。醤油が焦げないように気を付ける。

3. 器に盛っていりごまを散らす。

POTATO *KIMPIRA* WITH BACON

For this dish potatoes are cut into sticks and sautéed with bacon until tender but still slightly crunchy. Parsnips are also good cooked this way.

INGREDIENTS Serves Two

2 medium all-purpose potatoes
2 slices bacon
1 Tbsp vegetable oil
$1/2$ tsp crushed chili pepper
1 Tbsp soy sauce
1 Tbsp sugar
1 Tbsp water
$1/2$ tsp toasted sesame seeds
1 scallion, chopped
Ground black pepper

1 Wash and peel the potatoes. Cut lengthwise into ¼ in. (7 mm) slices, and cut each slice into ¼ in. (7 mm) sticks. Chop the bacon roughly.

2 Place the vegetable oil, bacon, and crushed chili pepper in a frying pan over medium heat and cook until the bacon fat renders out. Add the potato, soy sauce, sugar, and water, and cook until the liquid is almost gone. Turn off the heat, sprinkle with the sesame seeds, and stir once.

3 Arrange the potato *kimpira* in a serving bowl and top with the chopped scallions and ground black pepper.

じゃがいもと
ベーコンのきんぴら

2人分
じゃがいも　2個
ベーコンスライス　2枚
植物油　大さじ1
唐辛子（みじん切り）　小さじ1/2
醤油　大さじ1
砂糖　大さじ1
水　大さじ1
いりごま　小さじ1/2
細ねぎ（みじん切り）　1本分
黒こしょう　適量

1 じゃがいもは皮をむき、7mmの輪切りにしてから7mmの棒状に切る。ベーコンは粗みじん切りにする。

2 中火から強火で油を熱し、ベーコンと唐辛子をベーコンから脂が出るまで炒める。じゃがいも、醤油、砂糖、水を加え、汁気がほとんどなくなるまでさらに炒める。火を止め、いりごまを入れてひと混ぜする。

3 器に盛って細ねぎをのせ、黒こしょうをふる。

CHICKEN AND VEGETABLE STEW

The best part of this dish is not the chicken, but rather the nutritious root vegetables, which soak up the savory chicken and mushroom juices.

INGREDIENTS

Serves Two

- 5 1/2 oz. (160 g) chicken breast
- 1/2 medium carrot, peeled
- 2 in. (5 cm) length lotus root, about 1 oz. (30 g), peeled (optional)
- 2 large fresh *shiitake* mushrooms
- 6 snow peas, stems and strings removed
- 2 cups (480 ml) water
- 3 Tbsp soy sauce
- 1 1/2 Tbsp sugar
- 2 tsp vegetable oil
- 1 tsp toasted sesame seeds

1 Cut the chicken, carrot, and lotus root (if using) into bite-sized pieces. Remove the stem of each mushroom and cut in half.

2 Place the vegetable oil in a saucepan over medium-high heat. Add the chicken, carrot, lotus root, and mushrooms and sauté for 2 to 3 minutes. Add the water, soy sauce, and sugar, and bring to a simmer, then lower the heat and continue to simmer until the liquid is reduced, but enough remains to cook the snow peas. Add the peas and cook until tender. The liquid should be almost gone.

3 Arrange all ingredients in a serving bowl and sprinkle with the toasted sesame seeds.

● Other root vegetables such as parsnips, rutabaga, burdock root, or bamboo shoots can also be used if lotus root is not available.

筑前煮

2人分

鶏胸肉　160g
にんじん　1/2本
れんこん（好みで）　30g
しいたけ　大2枚
さやえんどう（筋を取る）　6個
水　2カップ
醤油　大さじ3
砂糖　大さじ1 1/2
植物油　小さじ2
いりごま　小さじ1

1 鶏肉、にんじん、れんこん（好みで）を一口大に切る。しいたけは軸を除いて汚れをふき、半分に切る。

2 中火から強火に油を熱する。鶏肉、にんじん、れんこん、しいたけを2〜3分炒める。水、醤油、砂糖を加えて煮立てる。火を弱め、汁気がなくなるまで煮る。さやえんどうを入れ、やわらかくなり、汁気がほとんどなくなるまでさらに煮る。

3 器に盛り、いりごまを散らす。

れんこんのかわりに、パースニップ、ルタバガ（スウェーデンカブ）、ごぼう、たけのこなどでもよいでしょう。

Dashi 2 / だし2

A richly-flavored stock can be obtained easily from available ingredients even without using *kombu*, bonito flakes etc.

昆布やかつおぶしを使わなくても、身近な材料でうま味たっぷりのだしを簡単にとることができます。

CHICKEN AND DRIED TOMATO BROTH

Sprinkling the chicken with salt and letting it sit for one hour will triple or quadruple its flavorful amino acid content. Dried tomatoes should be washed briefly in water to remove some of the off flavors that they acquire during the drying process.

INGREDIENTS — makes scant 1.8 quarts (1.8 l)

- 1 oz. (30 g) dried tomatoes
- 1 cup (240 ml) water
- 1 lb. (450 g) chicken breast, skinless
- 2 tsp salt
- 2 qts. (2 L) water

1. Briefly rinse the dried tomatoes in cold running water. Rehydrate in 1 cup water for 4 hours. Strain, reserving the soaking water.
2. Cut the chicken breast into thin slices and place in a bowl. Sprinkle with the salt, mix, and leave for 1 hour in refrigerator. The chicken will release its juices and then reabsorb them, becoming soft and a bit slippery.
3. Combine the water and chicken breast in a pot and bring to a simmer. Lower the heat, and maintain a bare simmer, with only one or two bubbles rising from the bottom of the pan, for 6 to 8 minutes. Skim the broth from time to time. Strain through a sieve.
4. Combine the dried tomato stock and the chicken breast stock.

鶏とドライトマトのだし

鶏肉に塩をまぶして1時間ほどおくと、うま味たっぷりのアミノ酸が何倍にも増えます。ドライトマトは水でさっと洗い、トマトを干すときに付く臭みを取り除きましょう。

できあがり 1.8ℓ

- ドライトマト　30g
- 水　1カップ
- 鶏胸肉（皮なし）　450g
- 塩　小さじ2
- 水　2ℓ

1. ドライトマトは流水で軽くすすぐ。1カップの水に4時間漬けて戻す。こして、漬け汁は取っておく。
2. 鶏肉は薄切りにしてボウルに入れる。塩をふって混ぜ、冷蔵庫で1時間おく。こうすることでやわらかくなる。
3. 鍋に水と鶏肉を入れて煮立てる。泡が少し立つぐらいの火加減に弱め、ときどきあくをすくいながら6〜8分煮る。ざるでこす。
4. ドライトマトを漬けた汁と鶏肉のだしを合わせる。

Chapter 6

Hot Pots

鍋もの 【*Nabemono*】

Japanese hot pots are comforting and warming in the winter,
yet light enough to be enjoyed in the heat of summer as well.
Hot pots allow couples or families to share the same simmering pot,
a communal experience that brings people a little closer.

寒い季節の鍋ものはからだが暖まりますが、
夏にもおいしくいただけます。
一緒に鍋を囲むと、親しさも深まります。

SUKIYAKI

I add tomatoes to sukiyaki for their fresh *umami* flavor.
If you are not comfortable with raw egg, omit it.

INGREDIENTS

Serves Two

- ½ block firm tofu or grilled tofu (*yaki-tofu*), about 6 oz. (170 g)
- 1 onion, peeled, halved, and thickly sliced
- 2 tomatoes, halved and thickly sliced
- ½ bunch fresh spinach, about 3 ½ oz. (100 g), cut into 2 in. (5 cm) lengths
- 2 large fresh *shiitake* mushrooms, cleaned and stems trimmed
- 1 Japanese long onion (*naganegi*), thinly sliced on the diagonal (optional)
- 1 pack (7 oz. / 200 g) *konnyaku* noodles (optional, also called *shirataki*)
- 7 oz. (200 g) top-quality beef, thinly sliced

Sukiyaki sauce:
- ½ cup (120 ml) soy sauce
- ¼ cup (50 g) sugar
- 1 cup (240 ml) water

- 2 eggs, for dipping

1 Cut the tofu into 8 pieces. Blanch and drain the konnyaku noodles (if using), and cut them into bite-sized pieces.

2 Arrange the beef, vegetables, and konnyaku noodles in a large pot. Combine all the sukiyaki sauce ingredients in a small bowl and pour over the beef and vegetables. Turn on the heat and bring to a simmer. (This can also be done directly on the table with a portable gas burner.)

3 Crack the eggs into individual bowls and beat. To eat, pick up pieces of cooked beef and vegetables with chopsticks, dip into the beaten egg, and eat.

● If you can't find thinly sliced beef, ask your butcher to cut ribeye or strip loin steak into paper-thin slices.

牛薄切り肉が手に入らなければ、リブロースかサーロインを精肉店でごく薄く切ってもらいましょう。

すき焼き

2人分

豆腐（木綿。または焼き豆腐）
　½丁（170g）
たまねぎ（半分にしてから厚切り）
　1個
トマト（半分にしてから厚切り）
　2個
ほうれん草（5cmに切る）
　½束（100g）
しいたけ（軸を除き、汚れをふく）
　大2枚
長ねぎ（斜め薄切り。好みで）　1本
白滝（好みで）　1袋
牛薄切り肉　200g
［すき焼きのたれ］
- 醤油　½カップ
- 砂糖　¼カップ
- 水　1カップ

卵　2個

1 豆腐は8等分に切る。白滝を入れる場合は湯通しして水気をきり、食べやすく切る。

2 鍋に牛肉、野菜、白滝、豆腐を入れる。すき焼きのたれを混ぜてかける。火を付けて煮立てる（卓上コンロで作ってもよい）。

3 それぞれの器に卵を溶く。具が煮えたらはしで取り分け、卵に付けて食べる。

SHABU-SHABU HOT POT

"*Shabu-shabu*" takes its name from the sound of the beef being swished through the hot pot. The vegetables may be cooked a bit longer, but the beef should stay in the broth only briefly.

INGREDIENTS   Serves Two

Ponzu sauce:
- ¼ cup (60 ml) soy sauce
- 2 Tbsp lemon juice
- 2 Tbsp vinegar
- 1 Tbsp sugar

Peanut sauce:
- 1 Tbsp peanut butter
- 1 Tbsp soy sauce
- 1 Tbsp lemon juice
- 2 tsp sugar

7 oz. (200 g) top-quality beef, thinly sliced
½ block tofu, 6 oz. (170 g)
½ head iceberg lettuce
⅓ medium carrot
2 large fresh *shiitake* mushrooms
1 oz. (30 g) *enoki* mushrooms (optional)
1 cup (240 ml) chicken broth
2½ cups (600 ml) water

1 Make the ponzu and peanut sauces ahead of time: combine the ingredients of each in separate bowls and set aside.

2 Cut the tofu into large chunks. Cut the lettuce into bite-sized pieces. Peel the carrot and cut into thin rounds. Trim the stems from the mushrooms. Arrange the beef, tofu, lettuce, carrot and mushrooms on a serving plate.

3 Set a portable gas burner on the dining table. Place a medium saucepan or shallow pot on the burner, pour in the chicken broth and water, and bring to a simmer. Add the ingredients, starting with those that take longer to cook such as carrots, and ending with the beef. Use chopsticks to take out vegetables and meat as they are cooked, dip them in either kind of sauce, and eat.

しゃぶしゃぶ

2人分
［ポン酢だれ］
- 醤油　¼カップ
- レモン汁　大さじ2
- 酢　大さじ2
- 砂糖　大さじ1

［ピーナツだれ］
- ピーナツバター　大さじ1
- 醤油　大さじ1
- レモン汁　大さじ1
- 砂糖　小さじ2

牛薄切り肉　200g
豆腐　½丁（170g）
アイスバーグレタス　½個
にんじん　⅓本
しいたけ（軸を除き、汚れをふく）
　　大2枚
えのき（好みで）　30g
チキンスープ　1カップ
水　2½カップ

1 材料をすべて混ぜ、ポン酢だれとピーナツだれを準備する。

2 豆腐は大きめに、レタスは一口大に切る。にんじんは皮をむいて薄い輪切りにする。肉、豆腐、野菜、しいたけを器にのせる。

3 卓上コンロに鍋を置き、チキンスープと水を入れて煮立てる。にんじんなど火が通りにくい材料から入れ、牛肉は最後に入れる。具が煮えたらはしで取り分け、ポン酢だれかピーナツだれに付けて食べる。

CHICKEN MEATBALL HOT POT

The fragrance of ginger in the chicken meatballs and the napa cabbage makes for a warming soup that is just slightly exotic.

INGREDIENTS

Serves Two to Three

Chicken meatballs:
- 11 oz. (310 g) ground chicken
- 1 scallion, finely chopped
- 1 small knob ginger, peeled and finely chopped
- ½ egg, beaten
- 1 Tbsp soy sauce
- 1 Tbsp potato starch or cornstarch

2 ½ cups (600 ml) water

2 Tbsp soy sauce

Pinch salt

⅛ napa cabbage, chopped

3 ½ oz. (100 g) spinach or garlic chives (also called *nira*), chopped

Crushed chili pepper (or *shichimi* spice powder)

1 Combine all the chicken meatball ingredients in a large bowl.

2 Pour the water into a large pan and bring to a simmer over medium heat. When the water is simmering, scoop up heaping tablespoons of the chicken meatball mixture, form them into balls, and add to the pan, maintaining a simmer. Use all the meatball mixture. Simmer until the chicken meatballs are cooked through.

3 Season to taste with soy sauce and salt, then add the napa cabbage and spinach or garlic chives. Cover and cook until tender.

4 Arrange the chicken meatballs, vegetables, and soup in individual bowls. Top with crushed chili pepper.

鶏だんご鍋

2〜3人分

[鶏だんご]
- 鶏ひき肉　310g
- 細ねぎ（みじん切り）　1本分
- しょうが（みじん切り）　1片分
- 溶き卵　1/2個分
- 醤油　大さじ1
- 片栗粉（またはコーンスターチ）　大さじ1

水　2 1/2カップ

醤油　大さじ2

塩　ひとつまみ

白菜　1/8個

ほうれん草（またはにら）　100g

唐辛子（みじん切り。または七味唐辛子）　適量

1 ボウルに鶏だんごの材料を入れてよく練る。

2 鍋に水を入れて中火で煮立てる。鶏肉をスプーンでだんごにすくって加える。だんごをすべて入れ、火が通るまで煮る。

3 醤油と塩で味を整える。きざんだ白菜とほうれん草（またはにら）を入れ、ふたをしてやわらかくなるまで煮る。

4 鶏だんごと野菜を汁ごと取り分け用の器によそい、唐辛子をふる。

SALMON AND *MISO* HOT POT

This is a nourishing family recipe with salmon, *miso*, potatoes and other vegetables. A pat of butter added at the last minute enhances the sweet umami of the salmon.

INGREDIENTS

Serves Two

- 7 oz. (200 g) fresh salmon, skin removed
- 1/4 head cabbage
- 1 large all-purpose potato
- 4 green beans
- 2 large fresh *shiitake* mushrooms
- 1 oz. (30 g) *enoki* mushrooms (optional)
- 1/2 cup (120 ml) chicken broth
- 1 1/2 cups (360 ml) water
- 2 Tbsp yellow *miso*
- 1 Tbsp butter

1 Cut the salmon into bite-sized pieces. Peel the potato, cut into 1/2 in. (1 cm) thick rounds, blanch and drain. Cut the cabbage and green beans into bite-sized pieces. Trim the stems from the mushrooms.

2 Pour the chicken broth and water into a large pan and mix in the *miso*. Add the salmon and vegetables to the pot, cover, and bring to a simmer. (This can also be done at the table with a portable gas burner.) When the salmon and vegetables are cooked, add the butter and let it melt halfway before serving the hot pot.

鮭の味噌鍋

2人分

鮭(皮を除く) 200g
キャベツ 1/4個
じゃがいも 大1個
いんげん 4本
しいたけ(軸を除き、汚れをふく) 大2枚
えのき(好みで) 30g
チキンスープ 1/2カップ
水 1 1/2カップ
味噌 大さじ2
バター 大さじ1

1 鮭は一口大に切る。じゃがいもは皮をむいて1cmの輪切りにする。ゆでて水気をきる。キャベツ、いんげんは一口大に切る。

2 鍋にチキンスープと水を入れて味噌を溶く。鮭と野菜を加え、ふたをして煮立てる(卓上コンロで作ってもよい)。鮭と野菜が煮えたらバターを加え、バターが半分ほど溶けたところで取り分け用の器によそう。

> **Rice 1 / ご飯 1**
>
> For Japanese cooking, use short-grain rice. When cooked, short-grain rice become moist and cohesive, while remaining airy and light.
>
> 和食には短粒米をお勧めします。粘りがあり、ふっくらとします。

COOKED RICE

The amount of water needed for cooking rice depends upon the humidity of the dry rice, the strength of the heat source, and the size and material of the cooking pot. Please note that following method and amounts are just a starting point. If the rice turns out too hard and dry, increase the water by a tablespoon and try again. If the rice turns out soggy or mushy, decrease the water by a tablespoon.

INGREDIENTS makes about 4 ¾ cups (880 g) cooked rice

2 cups (400 g) short-grain rice
2 cups plus 2 Tbsp water (510 ml)

1 Working in a sink, place the rice in a large bowl and add enough water to cover the rice by 1 in. (2.5 cm). Swish the rice around by hand for a few seconds; the water will become cloudy. Pour off the water immediately, placing one hand on the rice to keep it from spilling out of the bowl.

2 Pour in water just to cover the rice and swish by hand. When the water becomes cloudy, pour it off. Repeat three or four times. It's fine if the water is still a little cloudy.

3 Drain the rice in a sieve, then place in a medium saucepan with 2 cups plus 2 Tbsp water and allow to soak for 20 minutes.

4 Turn the heat to medium, cover, and bring to a boil. The water ideally should come to a boil in 5 to 10 minutes. Once it comes to a boil, immediately decrease the heat to very low and cook for 15 minutes.

5 Turn off the heat and leave undisturbed for 10 minutes. Uncover, and using a large spoon, bring the rice up from the bottom of the pot to the top, releasing steam and aerating the rice.

ご飯

米の乾燥度や熱源、鍋の材質によって水の量は変わりますので、下記の方法や分量は目安として調整してください。炊きあがったご飯が固すぎるようなら、大さじ1の水を加えてやり直してみましょう。逆にやわらかすぎるようなら、大さじ1の水を減らしてみてください。

できあがり 約4 ¾ カップ（880g）
短粒米　2カップ（400g）
水　2カップと大さじ2（510ml）

1 流しに大きめのボウルを置き、米を入れる。米がかぶるぐらいの水を注ぎ、片手で数秒勢いよくとぐ。水が濁ったらすぐ。

2 水に少し濁りが残るぐらいで、同様にして数回とぐ。

3 目の細かいざるに米をあけ、水気をきる。鍋に移し、水2カップと大さじ2を入れて20分おく。

4 鍋のふたをして中火にかけ、沸騰させる。沸騰したらごく弱火にして15分炊く。

5 火を止め、10分おく。ふたを開け、しゃもじなどで全体を返す。こうすることで余分な蒸気が抜け、ふっくらとする。

Chapter *7*

Rice and Noodles

ご飯と麺【*Gohan and Men*】

A bowl of rice or noodles can be a quick and easy meal for either lunch or dinner. For directions on washing and cooking white rice in a regular pot, see left page.

どんぶりものや麺類は、昼食にも夕食にも手早くできます。
鍋でのご飯の炊き方は、左ページをご参照ください。

MARINATED TUNA ON RICE

Tuna marinated in soy sauce on a bowl of hot rice is a healthy and satisfying full meal. If you can't find radish sprouts, use alfalfa sprouts or chopped scallions.

INGREDIENTS   Serves Two

3 cups hot cooked rice, about 1 lb. (450g)

Marinade:
- 3 Tbsp soy sauce
- 3 Tbsp *sake*
- 1 ½ Tbsp sugar
- 1 ½ Tbsp *wasabi* paste

7 oz. (200 g) *sashimi*-grade tuna, as fresh as possible

2 in. (5 cm) length *daikon* radish

1 cup (33 g) trimmed radish sprouts or chopped scallions, lightly packed

1 To make the marinade, combine the soy sauce, sake, and sugar in a medium saucepan, bring to a simmer and remove from heat. When cooled, mix in the wasabi paste.

2 Cut the fresh tuna into slices and soak in the pan of marinade for 5 minutes. Meanwhile, peel and grate the *daikon* radish. Place in a sieve and allow to drain for 2 to 3 minutes.

3 Arrange the rice in individual bowls and top with the marinated tuna slices. Mix some marinade in with the grated daikon radish to make a loose sauce. Spoon the sauce over the rice and tuna. Garnish with the radish sprouts.

まぐろの漬け丼

2人分

ご飯　450g

［漬け汁］
- 醤油　大さじ3
- 酒　大さじ3
- 砂糖　大さじ1½
- わさび　大さじ1½

まぐろ刺身　200g

大根おろし　5cm分

かいわれ大根（または細ねぎの
　みじん切り）　33g

1 醤油、酒、砂糖を鍋で煮立てる。火からはずし、冷めたらわさびを混ぜる。

2 まぐろの刺身を薄切りにして漬け汁に入れ、5分おく。大根おろしはざるに入れて2〜3分おき、水気をきる。

3 それぞれの丼にご飯をよそい、まぐろをのせる。大根おろしに漬け汁を少し混ぜ、ご飯とまぐろにかける。かいわれ大根を添える。

CHICKEN AND MUSHROOM RICE

Delicious and easy to make, this dish features chicken and mushrooms mixed into cooked white rice.

INGREDIENTS — Serves two to three

- 4 cups hot cooked rice, about 1 1/3 lbs. (600 g)
- 1 cup plus 3 Tbsp (285 ml) water
- 3 Tbsp soy sauce
- 3 Tbsp sugar
- 6 oz. (170 g) chicken breast, cut into bite-sized pieces
- 6 oz. (170 g) fresh mushrooms, wiped, trimmed and cut into 1/4 in. (5 mm) cubes
- 1 large knob ginger, peeled and grated
- 2 tsp toasted sesame seeds
- 1 scallion, chopped
- Finely diced lemon peel
- 10 leaves bibb lettuce (optional)

1 Combine the water, soy sauce, and sugar in a small pan and add the chicken and mushrooms. Bring to a simmer and cook until the liquid is almost gone. Turn off the heat and mix in the ginger, sesame seeds, scallions, and lemon peel.

2 Gently mix the rice and all the ingredients from step 1 in a large bowl. Arrange in individual bowls or on a serving plate lined with the bibb lettuce, if using.

● Choose a few different kinds of mushrooms that are good for cooking and combine them. Here I used 2 large *shiitake*, 2 oz. (60 g) *maitake*, and 2 oz. (60 g) *shimeji* mushrooms.

鶏肉とマッシュルームの混ぜご飯

2〜3人分
ご飯　600g
水　1カップと大さじ3
醤油　大さじ3
砂糖　大さじ3
鶏胸肉（一口大に切る）　170g
マッシュルーム（軸を除き、汚れをふく。5mm角に切る）　170g
おろししょうが　大1片分
いりごま　小さじ2
細ねぎ（みじん切り）　1本分
レモンの皮（細かいみじん切り）
　適量
ビブレタス（好みで）　10枚

1 水、醤油、砂糖を小鍋に入れ、鶏肉とマッシュルームを加えて煮立てる。汁気がほとんどなくなるまで煮たら火を止める。おろししょうが、いりごま、細ねぎ、レモンの皮を混ぜる。

2 大きめのボウルでご飯と**1**を混ぜる。それぞれの丼または器に好みでレタスを敷いて盛る。

数種類のきのこを混ぜて使ってもおいしくできます。今回はしいたけ大2枚、まいたけとしめじ各60gを混ぜて使いました。

SMOKED SALMON, BUTTER, AND SOY SAUCE ON RICE

This is one of my favorites. It's especially great when you're hungry and want to prepare a meal as quickly as possible.

INGREDIENTS

Serves Two

3 cups hot cooked rice, about 1 lb. (450 g)
6 $\frac{1}{2}$ oz. (180 g) thinly sliced smoked salmon
2 pieces butter, each $\frac{1}{2}$ Tbsp (7.5 g)
2 Tbsp soy sauce
$\frac{1}{4}$ onion, thinly sliced
2 pinches radish sprouts (optional)
Curly parsley for topping

Arrange the hot rice in individual bowls, top with butter, and sprinkle with soy sauce. Place the onion slices and radish sprouts (if using) over half of the rice, then lay the smoked salmon slices on the other half. Top with curly parsley.

スモークサーモンの
バター醤油丼

2人分

ご飯　450g
スモークサーモン（薄切り）　180g
バター　2かけ（各大さじ1/2）
醤油　大さじ2
たまねぎ（薄切り）　1/4個
かいわれ大根（好みで）　2つまみ
パセリ（飾り用）　適量

それぞれの丼にご飯をよそう。バターをのせ、醤油をかける。たまねぎと（好みで）かいわれ大根をご飯の半分にのせ、もう半分にスモークサーモンをのせる。パセリを飾る。

CHICKEN AND EGG ON RICE

The egg thickens the seasoned chicken broth in this dish so that it clings to the rice, making a hot and comforting lunch.

INGREDIENTS

Serves Two

3 cups hot cooked rice, about 1 lb. (450 g)
1 Tbsp chicken broth
4 Tbsp water
2 Tbsp soy sauce
1 Tbsp plus 2 tsp sugar
7 oz. (200 g) chicken breast, cut into bite-sized pieces
½ onion, thinly sliced
6 eggs, beaten
2 scallions, chopped, for topping
Crushed chili pepper (or *shichimi* spice powder)

1 Combine the chicken broth, water, soy sauce and sugar in a medium saucepan or frying pan. Add the chicken and onion and bring to a simmer over high heat. Simmer until the chicken is just cooked through. Pour in the beaten egg slowly, reduce the heat to low, and cook the egg to desired doneness by shaking the pan without stirring. (It's best if it's still a little runny.)

2 Arrange the rice in individual bowls and ladle the egg-and-chicken mixture over top. Garnish with chopped scallions and crushed chili pepper.

親子丼

2人分
ご飯　450g
チキンスープ　大さじ1
水　大さじ4
醤油　大さじ2
砂糖　大さじ1と小さじ2
鶏胸肉（一口大に切る）　200g
たまねぎ（薄切り）　½個
溶き卵　6個分
細ねぎ（みじん切り）　2本分
唐辛子（みじん切り。または七味唐辛子）　適量

1 鍋にチキンスープ、水、醤油、砂糖を入れる。鶏肉とたまねぎを加えて強火で煮立て、鶏肉に火が通るまで煮る。溶き卵を静かに入れ、弱火にして鍋を軽くゆすりながら、卵が好みの固さになるまで煮る（とろっとした状態が最適）。

2 それぞれの丼にご飯をよそい、卵と鶏肉をのせる。細ねぎをのせ、唐辛子をふる。

FRIED RICE

My favorite fried rice is made with eggs, scallions, ginger, sesame seeds, and soy sauce. I mix the beaten eggs with the rice before frying so that the flavors mingle better.

INGREDIENTS   Serves two to three

4 cups hot cooked rice, about 1 1/3 lbs. (600 g)

2 eggs, beaten

2 Tbsp vegetable oil

1 bunch scallions, chopped

1 small knob ginger, peeled and chopped

1 Tbsp soy sauce

1/2 cup (5 g) lightly packed dried bonito flakes (optional)

2 Tbsp toasted sesame seeds

1 Tbsp soy sauce for sprinkling

3 *shiso* leaves, minced,
   or a small bunch of cilantro leaves (optional)

1 Combine the cooked rice and beaten eggs in a bowl.

2 Heat the vegetable oil in a large frying pan or well-seasoned wok, add the scallions and ginger, and cook until the scallions are soft. Add the cooked rice and stir-fry until hot. Add the soy sauce and bonito flakes (if using), and stir-fry until the rice is dry and fluffy. To finish, sprinkle with sesame seeds and soy sauce, stir once and remove from heat.

3 Serve topped with the minced *shiso* leaves or cilantro (if using).

炒飯

2〜3人分

ご飯　600 g

溶き卵　2個分

植物油　大さじ2

細ねぎ（みじん切り）　1束分

しょうが（みじん切り）　1片分

醤油　大さじ1

かつおぶし（好みで）　5 g

いりごま　大さじ2

醤油（後で加える）　大さじ1

青じそ　3枚分
　またはコリアンダー（好みで）
　小1束

1 ご飯と溶き卵を混ぜる。

2 大きなフライパンか使いなれた中華鍋に油を熱して、細ねぎとしょうがを入れ、ねぎがしんなりするまで炒める。ご飯を加えて強火で炒める。醤油、好みでかつおぶしを加え、ご飯がぱらっとするまで炒める。いりごまと醤油をかけ、ひと炒めして火を止める。

3 好みで千切りにした青じそ（またはコリアンダー）を散らす。

SUSHI RICE BOWL

We serve this dish at home when celebrating a special occasion.
You can add or omit any ingredients as you wish.

INGREDIENTS

Serves two to three

4 cups sushi rice, about 1 $\frac{1}{3}$ lbs. (600 g) (see page 126)
1 tsp toasted sesame seeds
1 small knob ginger, peeled and grated
2 tsp minced lemon peel
$\frac{1}{4}$ small head iceberg lettuce, finely chopped
2 tsp (or more) *wasabi* paste
Topping suggestions:
- $\frac{1}{4}$ small onion
- $\frac{1}{2}$ avocado (and lemon juice for sprinkling)
- Rolled omelet (see page 36), made from 1 egg
- $\frac{1}{2}$ Japanese cucumber or $\frac{1}{4}$ peeled and seeded English cucumber
- 1 $\frac{1}{2}$ oz. (40 g) fresh tuna
- 1 $\frac{1}{2}$ oz. (40 g) smoked salmon
- 2 large cooked shrimp
- 2 Tbsp *ikura* salmon roe

1 For the toppings, cut each ingredient except the onion into $\frac{1}{2}$ in. (1 cm) cubes. Slice the onion very thinly. You may want to sprinkle lemon juice over the avocado to keep it from turning brown.

2 Combine the sushi rice with the toasted sesame seeds, ginger, lemon peel, lettuce, and wasabi in a large bowl. To mix, do not stir vigorously, but gently combine all ingredients by flipping the rice from the bottom to the top and cutting the seasonings into the rice with the edge of a flat spoon or paddle.

3 Place the seasoned rice in individual bowls and add your choice of toppings.

ちらし寿司

2〜3人分

寿司飯　600g（作り方はp.126）
いりごま　小さじ1
おろししょうが　1片分
レモンの皮（みじん切り）
　小さじ2
アイスバーグレタス（みじん切り）
　小 $\frac{1}{4}$ 個
わさび　小さじ2
［お勧めの具］
- たまねぎ　小 $\frac{1}{4}$ 個
- アボカド（レモン汁をかける）
  $\frac{1}{2}$ 個
- 巻き卵（作り方はp.36）
  卵1個分
- きゅうり　$\frac{1}{2}$ 本
  （イングリッシュ・キューカンバーなら　$\frac{1}{4}$ 本）
- まぐろ刺身　40g
- スモークサーモン　40g
- ゆでた海老　大2尾
- いくら　大さじ2

1 たまねぎはごく薄切りにし、それ以外の具は1cm角に切る（アボカドはレモン汁をかけると変色を防げる）。

2 寿司飯をボウルに入れ、いりごま、おろししょうが、レモンの皮、レタス、わさびを混ぜる。強く混ぜず、へらなどで底から上にご飯を返し、調味料がなじむようにする。

3 それぞれの丼に寿司飯を盛り、好みの具をのせる。

SUSHI HAND-ROLL WITH LETTUCE

When friends and family get together, everyone can enjoy assembling and rolling up sushi ingredients themselves and eating their creations. If you are familiar with nori seaweed, you can use it instead of lettuce.

| INGREDIENTS | Makes eight rolls |

3 cups sushi rice, about 1 lb. (450 g) (see page 126)

8 hand-sized leaves green-leaf lettuce

Wasabi paste

Filling suggestions:

- Fresh or smoked salmon, *ikura* salmon roe, and sliced onion
- Scrambled eggs and flying-fish roe (*tobiko*)
- Cooked shrimp, avocado, and mayonnaise
- Marinated tuna (see page 100), toasted sesame seeds and scallions

Lay out the rice, lettuce leaves, *wasabi* paste, and fillings separately on a table. To eat, each person should make their own roll by putting some of the sushi rice on a lettuce leaf, smearing the rice with a little *wasabi*, and rolling it all up with the filling of their choice.

手巻き寿司

8本分

寿司飯　450g（作り方はp.126）
グリーンリーフレタス　8枚
　（てのひらほどの大きさのもの）
わさび　適量
［お勧めの組み合わせ］
　鮭の刺身または
　　スモークサーモン、いくら、
　　たまねぎの薄切り
　炒り卵、とびこ（トビウオの卵
　　の塩漬け）
　ゆでた海老、アボカド、
　　マヨネーズ
　まぐろの漬け（作り方はp.100）、
　　いりごま、細ねぎ

寿司飯、レタス、わさび、具は別々の器に入れる。レタスに寿司飯を広げてわさびを塗る。好みの具を中央にのせ、手で巻く。

TUNA-MAYO RICE BALLS

Canned tuna is common in Japanese pantries, and tuna and mayonnaise rice balls are as popular in Japan as tuna salad sandwiches are in the West.

Put a quarter of the tuna-mayo mixture in the center of the rice.

ツナマヨネーズの1/4量を、ご飯の中央にのせる。

Roll the rice firmly into a log shape, but leave some air for a fluffier texture.

ラップにのせたご飯を筒型に整える。口あたりをよくするため、きつく巻きすぎない。

For this recipe, the sesame seeds should definitely be toasted for a richer flavor.

いりごまをまぶすと、香ばしい風味が楽しめる。

INGREDIENTS

Makes eight rice balls

A generous 3 cups hot cooked rice, about 17 oz. (480 g)
2 ½ oz. (70 g) canned tuna
2 heaping Tbsp mayonnaise
1 tsp soy sauce
1 scallion, chopped
3 Tbsp toasted sesame seeds

1 Drain the canned tuna and break up in a bowl. Add the mayonnaise, soy sauce, and chopped scallion and mix.

2 Roughly divide the rice into eighths and place one eighth on an 8 in. (20 cm) sheet of plastic wrap. Flatten the rice a little and place one fourth of the tuna mixture in the center. Cover with another eighth of the rice, and use the plastic wrap to roll into a log shape around the filling. Repeat with the remaining ingredients to make 4 logs.

3 Spread the toasted sesame seeds on a shallow dish. Unwrap the rice logs and roll them in the sesame seeds. Cut each log in half and arrange on a serving dish. Serve with your favorite pickled vegetables on the side (I use thinly sliced *daikon* pickles).

ツナマヨネーズ おにぎり

8個分

ご飯　480g
ツナ缶　70g
マヨネーズ　大さじ山盛り2
醤油　小さじ1
細ねぎ（みじん切り）　1本分
いりごま　大さじ3

1 ツナ缶の水気をきり、ボウルに入れる。マヨネーズ、醤油、細ねぎを加え、全体を混ぜる。

2 ご飯の1/8量を20cm角のラップに広げる。ツナの1/4量を中央にのせる。さらに1/8量のご飯をかぶせ、ラップで筒形になるよう形を整える。同様に4個作る。

3 皿にいりごまを入れ、ラップをはずしたご飯を転がしてごまをまぶす。同様に4個作り、それぞれ半分に切る。器に盛り、好みで漬物（大根など）を添える。

SEARED RICE BALLS WITH BACON SOY SAUCE

These rice balls can be grilled or broiled. The mouth-watering scent of toasted rice and warm soy sauce makes them irresistible.

Put a quarter of the bacon mixture in the center of the rice.

ベーコンの1/4量をご飯の中央にのせる。

Shape the rice firmly into a ball, but leave some air for a fluffier texture.

ラップで円盤形に整える。口あたりをよくするため、きつく握りすぎない。

Sear the rice balls to brown them slightly and brush with the soy sauce.

少し焦げ目がつくぐらいまで焼き、醤油を塗る。

INGREDIENTS — Makes four rice balls

A generous 3 cups hot cooked rice, about 17 oz. (480 g)

2 oz. (60 g) sliced bacon (about 2 regular slices), finely chopped

2 Tbsp soy sauce

4 Tbsp *sake*

1 Tbsp sugar

3 Tbsp minced lemon peel

1 Tbsp lemon juice

1 Tbsp toasted sesame seeds

1 tsp vegetable oil

Extra soy sauce for basting

1 Combine the bacon, soy sauce, *sake*, and sugar in a small saucepan and reduce over low heat, stirring frequently until, the liquid is gone. Remove from heat and add the lemon peel, lemon juice, and toasted sesame seeds.

2 Spread ¼ of the rice on an 8 in. (20 cm) sheet of plastic wrap, and place ¼ of the bacon mixture in the center of the rice. Use the plastic wrap to shape the rice into a ball around the bacon, and then flatten slightly to form a thick patty. Repeat with the remaining portions.

3 In a non-stick frying pan, heat the vegetable oil over a medium flame. Unwrap the rice balls and sear until well browned on both sides, brushing with extra soy sauce after searing. Serve alongside your favorite pickled vegetables (here I used a pickled *umeboshi* plum).

ベーコン入り焼きおにぎり

4個分

ご飯　480g
ベーコンスライス（みじん切り）
　60g
醤油　大さじ2
酒　大さじ4
砂糖　大さじ1
レモンの皮（細かいみじん切り）
　大さじ3
レモン汁　大さじ1
いりごま　大さじ1
植物油　小さじ1
醤油（塗る用）　適量

1 ベーコン、醤油、酒、砂糖を鍋に入れて弱火にかける。混ぜながら汁気を飛ばす。火からはずし、レモンの皮、レモン汁、いりごまを混ぜる。

2 ご飯の1/4量を20cm角のラップに広げる。ベーコンの1/4量を中央にのせる。ラップで巻き、円盤型に整える。残りも同様に作る。

3 フッ素樹脂加工のフライパンを中火にかけて油を熱する。ラップをはずしたご飯を両面がこんがりとするまで焼き、醤油をはけで塗る。器に盛り、好みで漬物（梅干しなど）を添える。

SOBA NOODLES WITH SWEET SOY SAUCE

Soba, traditional buckwheat noodles, are excellent served cold in a soy sauce-based broth with plenty of thinly sliced vegetables.

INGREDIENTS Serves Two

Sweet soy-sauce broth:
- ½ cup (60 ml) chicken broth
- 1 cup (240 ml) water
- 2 Tbsp soy sauce
- 1 Tbsp sugar

1 scallion, chopped
8 oz. (230 g) dried *soba* buckwheat noodles
¼ onion (preferably a sweet variety), thinly sliced
½ cup (16 g) lightly packed trimmed sprouts, any kind
½ tsp *wasabi* paste
2 large pinches dried bonito flakes (optional)

1 Combine the sweet soy-sauce broth ingredients in a small saucepan, bring to a simmer, and remove from heat. When cooled to room temperature, add the chopped scallion and set aside.

2 Bring a large pot of water to a boil. Add the *soba* noodles and cook according to the directions on the package. Drain the noodles and place immediately under cold running water to halt cooking. Drain very well and divide between individual bowls.

3 Arrange the sliced onion, sprouts, and a dab of mustard on top of the noodles in each bowl. Sprinkle with the dried bonito flakes, if using. Pour the broth over the noodles just before eating.

かけそば

2人分
[つゆ]
- チキンスープ　½カップ
- 水　1カップ
- 醤油　大さじ2
- 砂糖　大さじ1

細ねぎ（みじん切り）　1本分
そば（乾）　230ｇ
たまねぎ（薄切り）　¼個
かいわれ菜　16ｇ
わさび　小さじ½
かつおぶし（好みで）　2つまみ

1 つゆの材料を小鍋に入れて煮立て、火からはずす。室温になるまで冷まし、細ねぎを入れる。

2 たっぷりの湯を沸かし、表示に従ってそばをゆでる。水気をきり、そばをすばやく流水で洗う。よく水気をきり、それぞれの器に盛る。

3 薄切りにしたたまねぎとかいわれ菜、わさびをのせる。好みでかつおぶしを散らす。食べる直前につゆをかける。

CHICKEN AND ONION NOODLE SOUP

The best part of this soup is the scallions, so use the best, freshest green onions you can find.

INGREDIENTS	Serves Two

7 oz. (200 g) skinned chicken breast
1 tsp salt
1 bunch scallions, cut into 1 in. (2.5 cm) lengths
2 cups (480 ml) water
2 Tbsp soy sauce
1 tsp sugar
8 oz. (230 g) dried *soba* buckwheat noodles
Crushed chili pepper (or *shichimi* spice powder)

1 Slice the chicken breast thinly at a steep angle to make wide slices. Sprinkle the salt on the slices and leave for 15 minutes.

2 Put the salted chicken and water in a medium saucepan and bring to a simmer. Add the soy sauce, sugar and scallions and simmer until the scallions are soft.

3 Meanwhile, bring a large pot of water to a boil. Add the noodles and cook according to the directions on the package. Drain very well and divide between individual bowls.

4 Ladle the chicken, scallions, and soup over top and garnish with crushed chili pepper.

● Whole-wheat pasta can be substituted for *soba* buckwheat noodles.

鶏ねぎそば

2人分
鶏胸肉（皮なし）　200g
塩　小さじ1
細ねぎ（2.5cmに切る）　1束
水　2カップ
醤油　大さじ2
砂糖　小さじ1
そば（乾）　230g
唐辛子（みじん切り。または七味
　唐辛子）　適量

1 鶏肉は薄くそぎ切りにする。塩をふって15分おく。

2 鶏肉と水を鍋に入れて煮立てる。醤油、砂糖、細ねぎを入れてねぎがやわらかくなるまで煮る。

3 たっぷりの湯を沸かし、表示に従ってそばをゆでる。水気をよくきり、それぞれの器に盛る。

4 鶏肉とねぎを汁ごとそばにかけ、唐辛子をふる。

そばの代わりに全粒粉パスタでもよい。

FRIED NOODLES

Frying noodles is a Chinese technique, but I like to add a Japanese touch by using buckwheat noodles, tofu, and *sake*.

INGREDIENTS	Serves Two

- 3 ½ oz. (100 g) *abura-age* deep-fried tofu, thawed if frozen
- ½ bunch scallions
- 8 oz. (230 g) dried *soba* buckwheat noodles
- 1 Tbsp vegetable oil
- 3 Tbsp soy sauce
- 2 Tbsp *sake*
- 1 tsp sugar
- Crushed chili pepper (or *shichimi* spice powder)
- ½ cup (5 g) lightly packed dried bonito flakes (optional)

1 Cut the deep-fried tofu into bite-sized pieces. Cut the scallions into 1 in. (2.5 cm) lengths.

2 Bring a large pot of water to a boil. Add the noodles and cook according to the directions on the package. Drain very well.

3 Heat the oil in a large frying pan over high heat. Once the oil shimmers, add the deep-fried tofu and scallions and cook until the scallions are slightly soft. Add the cooked noodles and stir-fry for a minute or two. Add the *sake*, soy sauce and sugar and stir-fry until the liquid has disappeared.

4 Serve the fried noodles on individual plates; garnish with crushed chili pepper and bonito flakes (if using).

● Whole-wheat pasta can be substituted for *soba* buckwheat noodles.

焼きそば

2人分
油揚げ（冷凍の場合は解凍しておく）
　100g
細ねぎ　½束
そば（乾）　230g
植物油　大さじ1
醤油　大さじ3
酒　大さじ2
砂糖　小さじ1
唐辛子（みじん切り。または七味
　唐辛子）　適量
かつおぶし（好みで）　5g

1 油揚げは一口大に切る。細ねぎは2.5cmに切る。

2 たっぷりの湯を沸かし、表示に従ってそばをゆでる。水気をよくきる。

3 フライパンを強火にかけ、油を熱する。油揚げと細ねぎをねぎが少ししんなりするまで炒める。そばを入れて1〜2分したら、酒、醤油、砂糖を加えて汁気がなくなるまで強火で炒める。

4 それぞれの器に盛り、唐辛子と好みでかつおぶしを散らす。

そばの代わりに全粒粉パスタでもよい。

BEEF NOODLE SOUP

Udon, thick wheat noodles, are now widely available in the West.
If you can't find them, use any thick, substantial noodle.

INGREDIENTS

Serves Two

7 oz. (200 g) beef top round, thinly sliced
1 tsp salt
2½ cups (600 ml) water
3 Tbsp plus 1 tsp soy sauce
2 tsp sugar
1 bunch scallions, cut into 1 in. (2.5 cm) pieces
8 oz. (230 g) dried *udon* noodles
Crushed chili pepper (or *shichimi* spice powder)

1 Sprinkle the salt on the sliced beef and leave for 15 minutes.

2 Put the salted beef and water in a medium saucepan and bring to a simmer. Add the soy sauce, sugar and scallions and simmer until the scallions are soft.

3 Meanwhile, bring a large pot of water to a boil. Add the *udon* noodles and cook according to the directions on the package. Drain very well and divide between individual bowls. Ladle the beef, scallions, and soup over top and garnish with crushed chili pepper.

● You can substitute *soba* buckwheat noodles or whole wheat pasta for *udon* noodles.

肉うどん

2人分
牛薄切り肉　200ｇ
塩　小さじ1
水　2½カップ
醤油　大さじ3、小さじ1
砂糖　小さじ2
細ねぎ（2.5cmに切る）　1束
うどん（乾）　230ｇ
唐辛子（みじん切り。または七味唐辛子）　適量

1 牛肉に塩をふって15分おく。

2 牛肉と水を鍋に入れて煮立てる。醤油、砂糖、細ねぎを入れてねぎがやわらかくなるまで煮る。

3 たっぷりの湯を沸かし、表示に従ってうどんをゆでる。水気をよくきり、それぞれの器に盛る。牛肉とねぎを汁ごとうどんにかけ、唐辛子をふる。

うどんの代わりにそばや全粒粉パスタでもよい。

Rice 2
ご飯2

Instructions for preparing the sushi rice used on pp.110 and 112. The tartness of the rice makes it the perfect complement to seafood and vegetables.

p.110、112で使用した寿司飯の炊き方です。酸味のあるご飯は魚介や野菜とよく合います。

VINEGARED SUSHI RICE

Rice cooked for sushi should be slightly firmer in texture than regular cooked rice, so that it can absorb the seasoned vinegar added after cooking.

INGREDIENTS makes about 4 ¾ cups (880 g) cooked rice

Sushi vinegar:
- 3 ½ Tbsp rice vinegar
- 2 ½ Tbsp sugar
- 2 tsp salt

Just-cooked rice made from 2 cups (400 g) uncooked short-grain rice and 2 cups (480 ml) water (see directions on page 98)

1 While the rice is cooking, combine the rice vinegar, sugar, and salt in a non-reactive saucepan over medium-low heat. Stir constantly until the sugar and salt dissolve completely. Immediately turn off the heat.

2 Place the hot rice in a large bowl. Sprinkle with all of the sushi vinegar and mix with a flipping and cutting motion to evenly distribute the vinegar and aerate the rice.

寿司飯

寿司飯は普通のご飯より少し硬めに炊いたほうが、寿司酢がご飯によくなじみます。

できあがり 約4 ¾カップ（880g）

［寿司酢］
- 米酢　大さじ3 ½
- 砂糖　大さじ2 ½
- 塩　小さじ2

短粒米　2カップ（400g）
水　2カップ

1 ご飯を炊くあいだ、鍋（酸に強いもの）に寿司酢の材料を入れ、弱火から中火にかける。混ぜながら砂糖と塩を溶かし、火を止める。

2 ボウルに炊きたてのご飯を入れ、寿司酢を加える。しゃもじなどで切るようにして手早く全体を混ぜる。

Chapter 8

Soups

椀もの【*Wanmono*】

Soups are eaten throughout the course of the meal at the Japanese table, accompanying rice and other side dishes. Here are some simple yet hearty recipes that bring out the natural, wholesome flavors of their ingredients.

ご飯やおかずとともに、日本の食卓に椀ものは欠かせません。素材の風味がいかされた、簡単で温まるものをご紹介します。

EGG AND BACON SOUP

A hearty but delicate soup, with a pleasant
smoky aroma from the bacon.

INGREDIENTS Serves Two

2 cups (480 ml) water
1/8 onion, sliced
2 oz. (60 g) sliced bacon (about 2 regular slices), cut into pieces
2 eggs
1 Tbsp cornstarch
2 tsp soy sauce
Pinch salt
1 tsp parsley, chopped

1. Combine the water, onion, and bacon in a small saucepan and bring to a simmer. Meanwhile, beat the eggs and combine with the cornstarch. When the water simmers, add the soy sauce and salt. Pour in the egg mixture, stirring, and keep at a gentle simmer until the eggs set.

2. Ladle into individual bowls and top with the chopped parsley.

ベーコン入りかきたま汁

2人分
水　2カップ
たまねぎ（薄切り）　1/8個
ベーコンスライス（細切り）　60g
卵　2個
コーンスターチ　大さじ1
醤油　小さじ2
塩　ひとつまみ
パセリ（みじん切り）　小さじ1

1. 水、たまねぎ、ベーコンを鍋に入れて煮立てる。卵は溶いてコーンスターチを混ぜる。水が煮立ったら、醤油と塩を加える。静かに卵を流し入れ、軽くかき混ぜながら中火で卵に火が通るまで煮る。

2. それぞれの器に汁をよそう。パセリを散らす。

CHICKEN AND TOFU SOUP

This soup derives its umami from the chicken and tofu,
so you don't need to add broth to give it flavor.

INGREDIENTS Serves Two

6 oz. (170 g) boneless chicken thighs
1/3 block firm tofu, about 4 oz. (120 g)
1/3 medium carrot
4 in. (10 cm) stalk celery
2 Tbsp vegetable oil
2 cups (480 ml) water
Scant 1 tsp salt
1 Tbsp soy sauce
1/2 scallion, chopped
2 pinches crushed chili pepper (or *shichimi* spice powder)

1 Cut the chicken thighs into 1/2 in. (1 cm) cubes. Break up the tofu into coarse pieces. Cut the carrot and celery into thin sticks.

2 Put the oil in a saucepan over medium heat. Add the chicken, tofu, carrot and celery and sauté until the surface of the chicken changes color. Pour in the water, bring to a simmer and cook until the vegetables are tender. Season with salt and soy sauce.

3 Ladle into individual bowls and top with the chopped scallions and crushed chili pepper.

鶏の豆腐汁

2人分
鶏もも肉（皮なし） 170g
豆腐（木綿） 1/3丁（120g）
にんじん 1/3本
セロリ 10cm
植物油 大さじ2
水 2カップ
塩 小さじ1弱
醤油 大さじ1
細ねぎ（みじん切り） 1/2束分
唐辛子（みじん切り。または七味唐辛子） 2つまみ

1 鶏肉は1cm角に切る。豆腐は粗く崩す。にんじんとセロリは細い棒状に切る。

2 鍋を中火にかけて油を熱する。鶏肉、豆腐、にんじん、セロリを入れ、鶏肉の色が変わるまで炒める。水を注いで煮立て、野菜がやわらかくなるまで煮る。塩と醤油で味を整える。

3 器に汁をよそう。細ねぎをのせ、唐辛子をふる。

CLAM AND *MISO* SOUP

I like to use my favorite red *miso* made only with whole soybeans and salt for this soup, but try it with any kind of *miso* you can find.

INGREDIENTS	Serves Two

7 oz. (200 g) steamer clams, expelled of sand (see page 60)

2 cups (480 ml) water

2 Tbsp *miso* (any kind)

Pinch sugar

½ scallion, chopped

1 Combine the clams and water in a small saucepan and bring to a simmer. Cook until the clams open, then turn off the heat and stir in the *miso* and sugar.

2 Ladle clams and soup into individual bowls and top with the chopped scallions. When eating, use fingers and/or chopsticks to remove the meat from the shells.

あさりの味噌汁

2人分

あさり　200 g（砂抜きのやり方はp.60を参照）
水　2カップ
味噌　大さじ2
砂糖　ひとつまみ
細ねぎ（みじん切り）　1/2束分

1 小鍋にあさりと水を入れて煮立てる。あさりの口が開いたら火を止め、味噌と砂糖を溶かす。

2 それぞれの器にあさりと汁をよそい、細ねぎをのせる。あさりは指やはしで殻から身をはずして食べる。

Scoop the *miso* with a ladle, dip into the broth, and stir in the *miso* little by little.

Do not allow the soup to boil after adding the *miso* or it will become sour and unpleasant.

味噌はお玉などを使い、汁を入れながら少しずつ溶く。

風味が飛んでしまうので、味噌を入れたあとは汁を煮立たせないように気を付ける。

PORK AND ROOT VEGETABLE SOUP

Rich with pork and *miso*, this is a great soup for a cold winter day.

INGREDIENTS Serves Two

3 1/2 oz. (100 g) pork slices or cubes cut from loin, belly or ham
1/2 tsp salt
1 medium all-purpose potato
1/2 small onion
1/3 small carrot
2 tsp vegetable oil
1 2/3 cups (400 ml) water
2 Tbsp *miso*, any kind
1/2 scallion, chopped
2 pinches ground red pepper

1 Sprinkle the pork with the salt and leave for 15 minutes. Peel the potato, onion, and carrot and cut into small bite-sized pieces.

2 Heat the vegetable oil in a medium saucepan and add the carrot, potato, onion, and pork. Sauté until the pork is just cooked through. Pour in the water, bring to a simmer, and cook until the potato is tender. Stir in the *miso*. Do not allow the soup to boil after adding the miso.

3 Serve in individual bowls and top with the scallion and ground red pepper.

豚汁

2人分
豚薄切り肉（または腰肉、バラ肉、もも肉）　100g
塩　小さじ1/2
じゃがいも　1個
たまねぎ　小1/2個
にんじん　小1/3本
植物油　小さじ2
水　1 2/3カップ
味噌　大さじ2
細ねぎ（みじん切り）　1/2束分
粉唐辛子　2つまみ

1 豚肉に塩をふって15分おく。じゃがいも、たまねぎ、にんじんは皮をむき、小さめの一口大に切る。

2 鍋に油を熱し、にんじん、じゃがいも、たまねぎ、豚肉を入れる。肉に火が通るまで炒める。水を注いで煮立て、じゃがいもがやわらかくなるまで煮る。味噌を溶き入れたら、煮立たせないように注意する。

3 それぞれの器に汁をよそい、細ねぎをのせ、粉唐辛子をふる。

GLOSSARY 食材メモ

abura-age deep-fried tofu Firm tofu cut into thin sheets and deep-fried.

油揚げ　木綿豆腐を薄切りにして揚げたもの。

Anaheim pepper An American variety of mild chili pepper. In Japan, *manganji* or *fushimi* peppers are used. Any mild variety can be substituted, or use ordinary bell peppers.

アナハイム・ペッパー　米国産の辛みの弱い唐辛子。日本では万願寺唐辛子や伏見唐辛子が用いられる。他の辛みの弱い品種や普通のピーマンでも代用できる。

bonito flakes Dried flakes of *katsuo* (bonito or skipjack tuna) made by steaming, smoke-drying, and aging fillets of the fish until they are wood-hard, and then shredding them into flakes.

かつおぶし（削り）　かつおを煮たあとで燻し、乾燥させるなど加工してできた固いかつおぶしを、薄く削ったもの。

daikon radish A long white radish with a mild refreshing taste, good both raw (usually finely grated) and cooked.

大根　辛みが弱く、生でも食べられる。

dashi Japanese stock or broth used as a base for soups and sauces and to infuse umami into foods, usually made from dried kombu kelp and bonito flakes. There are other varieties of dashi made from dried small sardines, mackerel, and *shiitake* mushrooms. In fact, dashi can be made from any dried, umami-rich food: ham, dried mushrooms, dried tomatoes, and so on.

だし　椀ものや、つゆのベースとなったり、食材のうま味を増したりなど和食の素となる汁。主に干した昆布とかつおぶしからとる。干したいわしやさば、干ししいたけなどもよく使われる。ハム、乾燥マッシュルーム、ドライトマトなど、さまざまな食材からだしをとることができる。

enoki mushroom A long, white, noodle-shaped mushroom with a mild flavor.

えのき　くせがなく、あっさりとした味わい。

escabeche Fish and vegetables that have been deep-fried and marinated in vinegar, called *nambanzuke* in Japanese. Like tempura, escabeche came to Japan with the first Portuguese and Spanish explorers hundreds of years ago.

南蛮漬け　揚げた魚や野菜を酢漬けにしたもの。天ぷらと同様に17世紀にポルトガル人やスペイン人によって日本にもたらされた。

ikura salmon roe Cleaned and salted salmon roe. "Ikura" is originally a Russian word meaning fish roe.

いくら　鮭の卵を1粒ずつばらして塩漬けにしたもの。ロシア語で"魚の卵"を意味するIkuraが語源とされる。

kabocha squash A Japanese variety of winter squash, like a pumpkin but firmer and less watery. Kabocha has bright yellow-orange flesh and a hard, but thin and edible, dark green rind. The rind is often partially peeled to show off the contrast between the green skin and orange flesh.

かぼちゃ　身は黄色くみずみずしく、硬い緑色の皮まで食べることができる。黄色と緑の色合いを強調するため、わざと皮を少し残して調理することも多い。

kamaboko A kind of fish sausage or fish cake made by grinding the meat of several varieties of fish and mixing it with seasonings, curing it, and steaming it into different shapes and textures.

かまぼこ　主に白身魚をすりつぶし、塩分などを加えて蒸しあげ、加工した練りもの。

kanikamaboko Imitation crab legs made from kamaboko. Some kanikama products have real crab meat blended in with the kamaboko.

かにかまぼこ　色や形状をかにに似せて作ったかまぼこ。本物のかにの身を混ぜたものもある。

kimpira Shredded vegetables sautéed and seasoned with soy sauce, sugar (or *mirin*), chili peppers and sesame seeds. Burdock root and carrot is a common combination, but there are many variations.

きんぴら　野菜を細切りにして醤油、砂糖（またはみりん）、唐辛子、ごまで味つけをしたもの。ごぼうやにんじんが一般的だが、さまざまな食材で作られる。

kombu kelp A variety of giant kelp that is dried and used for dashi. Most Japanese kombu is grown off the coast of Hokkaido, the country's northernmost main island.

昆布　海藻の一種で、乾燥させたものはだしをとるのによく使われる。日本では、北海道沖が主な産地となっている。

konnyaku A very stiff, nearly flavorless white jelly made by grinding the root of the konnyaku (konjac) plant and coagulating it with calcium hydroxide. Another type, grayish brown in color, contains *hijiki* seaweed. Rich in fiber with almost no calories, konnyaku is sold in slabs or shaped into noodles called *shirataki*.

こんにゃく　こんにゃくいもをすりつぶして凝固させたもの。独特の食感を持ち、白灰色で味はほとんどない。ひじきなどの海藻を混ぜて黒っぽくしたものもある。カロリーがゼロに近く繊維質が豊富。板状または麺状（白滝）で売られている。

miso An intensely flavorful paste made from soybeans and rice or other grains, steamed and fermented with salt. Full of umami, miso comes in hundreds of local varieties.

味噌　大豆や米、麦などを蒸し、塩で発酵熟成させて作る。うま味に満ち、地域によってさまざまな種類がある。

panko bread crumbs Coarse white bread crumbs used for deep-frying in Japanese food. Panko is lighter than other commercial bread crumbs because it is made from bread without crusts.

パン粉　パンを細かく砕いて乾燥させたもの。揚げものの衣に使われる。パンの耳を使わないので軽い仕上がりになる。

rice vinegar Vinegar made by fermenting steamed rice with acetic acid bacteria. Slow-brewed rice vinegar is not merely sour, but has umami and other complex flavors and aromas. Essential for making sushi.

米酢　蒸米を酢酸発酵させて作った酢。時間をかけて発酵させた酢はまろやかで豊かなうま味と香りを持つ。寿司には欠かせない。

sake　An alcoholic beverage made by double-fermenting cooked rice; first to turn the starches into sugars, and then to turn the sugars into alcohol.

酒　蒸米を醸造して作る。蒸米は育成されて麹となり、米のでんぷんを糖分に変え、さらにアルコール発酵を促す。

shichimi spice powder　A Japanese spice mix often made by combining chili pepper flakes, sesame seeds, poppy seeds, *sansho* pepper, *nori* (seaweed), dried orange peel and other spices. There are many variations.

七味唐辛子　唐辛子、ごま、けしの実、山椒、のり、干したみかんの皮などの香辛料を調合した調味料。混ぜ合わせる香辛料には、さまざまなバリエーションがある。

shiitake mushroom　A mushroom native to China with a meaty, earthy flavor. Fresh shiitake are grilled, deep-fried, sautéed or stewed. Dried shiitake are used to make dashi.

しいたけ　中国原産で、肉のようなうま味を持つ。焼きもの、煮物、炒めもの、揚げものなど広く料理される。干したものはだしをとるのに使われる。

shirataki　See konnyaku.

白滝　こんにゃくを参照。

shiso leaves　A Japanese herb related to mint and basil, with an aroma like basil, but fresher and grassier. There is also a purple variety with a slightly different aroma that is used to color and flavor pickled vegetables.

しそ　日本の薬用植物。バジルに似た香りを持つが、より青々しい。茎や葉が赤紫の赤じそは、漬物の色づけに使われる。

soba buckwheat noodles　Noodles made from buckwheat flour. Different grades of soba are available, containing varying proportions of buckwheat and wheat flour.

そば　そば粉を主原料とし、そば粉と小麦粉の配合によってさまざまな種類がある。

soy sauce　A liquid condiment made by fermenting steamed soybeans with roasted wheat and salt. Like other Japanese essential seasonings such as rice vinegar and sake, good, slow-brewed soy sauce is mild but profound, full of umami and other flavors and aromas.

醤油　蒸した大豆、炒った小麦粉、塩などを混ぜて発酵させて作る。まろやかで深いうま味を持つ。

tempura　Seasonal vegetables and seafood battered with flour, egg, and water and deep-fried in hot oil, eaten with sea salt or with a dipping sauce based on soy sauce and dashi. Brought to Japan by the Portuguese almost five hundred years ago.

天ぷら　野菜や魚介類を卵、小麦粉、水を混ぜた衣を付けて揚げたもの。16世紀にポルトガル人によって日本に広まったとされる。

teriyaki A grilling technique in which fish or meat is basted and glazed with a mixture of sugar, soy sauce and sake while grilling or sautéing to add flavor and create a glossy shine.

照り焼き　醤油や砂糖、酒を基本としたたれを魚や肉に回しかけながら焼く調理法。焼くことで表面につや（照り）が出て風味も増す。

tofu Soy milk that has been coagulated into a dense, protein-rich solid. Good-quality tofu is tender and milky, not watery or rubbery, so look around a little for the best tofu you can find.

豆腐　豆乳を固めたもの。品質の良い豆腐は豆のうまみが強く、しっとりとしている。

umami A fifth taste, scientifically discovered in Japan but really known everywhere, sometimes called "savoriness." Umami receptors are located in the back of the tongue and are stimulated by free amino acids found in meats, seaweed, and certain vegetables like tomatoes and mushrooms. Curing or drying foods enhances their natural umami.

うま味　日本で解明された5つの基本味のひとつ。現在では広く知られている。肉、海藻、トマトやしいたけのような野菜に含まれるアミノ酸が、舌の味蕾にある感覚細胞を刺激することでうま味を感じる。燻製や干した食材はうま味が増す。

wasabi The root of a plant that grows near pure mountain streams, ground into a paste and eaten as a condiment on many foods, most notably sushi and sashimi. The paste has a hot, refreshing pungency, like strong mustard or horseradish. Wasabi sold in paste or powder form is usually mixed with horseradish, but is an acceptable substitute.

わさび　山間の水のきれいな渓流のそばに生え、栽培もされる植物。寿司や刺身をはじめ、多くの和食に薬味として添えられる。マスタードやホースラディッシュのようなピリッとした刺激を持つ。

yaki-tofu Tofu pressed with a very hot grill to create a firmer texture and blackened grill lines, used for sautéing and in hot pots.

焼き豆腐　豆腐をあぶって表面に焼き目をつけたもの。普通の豆腐よりくずれにくいため、炒めものや煮物に向いている。

INDEX

Bold type indicates an item that is defined in the glossary (pp.136–139).

A

***abura-age* deep-fried tofu** 123, **136**
Anaheim pepper 29, **136**
avocado 111, 113

B

baby salad greens 23, 27
bacon 23, 73, 75, 85, 117, 129
beef 27, 71, 91, 93, 125
bell pepper 33, 53
bonito flakes 29, 39, 68, 109, 119, 123, **136**
bread crumbs 47, 49, 137
broccoli 27
burdock root 45, 83, 87
butter 31, 97, 105

C

cabbage 35, 49, 97
calamari 79
carrot 45, 57, 63, 83, 87, 93, 131, 135
celery 21, 131
chervil 45, 65
chiken 33, 51, 57, 65, 77, 87, 88, 95, 103, 107, 121, 131
chili pepper 29, 33, 55, 57, 65, 79, 83, 85, 95, 107, 121, 123, 125, 131, 135
cilantro 109
clams 61, 133
cod 53

D

***daikon* radish** 21, 37, 55, 58, 79, 101, **136**
dashi 68, 88, **136**
dried tomatoes 88

E

egg(s) 37, 43, 47, 49, 51, 65, 95, 107, 109, 111, 113, 129
eggplant 39

***enoki* mashrooms** 67, 93, 97, **136**
escabeche 57, **136**

F

fava beans 17
flying-fish roe (*tobiko*) 113

G

garlic chives (*nira*) 95
ginger 35, 39, 51, 55, 58, 61, 81, 95, 103, 109, 111
green beans 15, 63, 79, 97
green peas 71

I

***ikura* salmon roe** 111, 113, **136**

J

Japanese cucumber 111
Japanese long onion (*naganegi*) 33, 91

K

***kabocha* squash** 45, 63, 75, **137**
kamaboko 21, **137**
kanikama 21, **137**
kimpira 83, 85, **137**
***kombu* kelp** 67, 68, **137**
konnyaku **137**
konnyaku noodles 91

L

lemon 21, 23, 27, 31, 47, 51, 53, 57, 65, 67, 73, 77, 93, 103, 111, 117
lettuce 47, 53, 93, 103, 111, 113
lotus root 87

M

mackerel 81
miso 97, 133, 135, **137**
mitsuba herb 65

mushroom   *67, 103*

N

napa cabbage   *73, 95*

O

onion   *23, 33, 57, 91, 105, 107, 111, 113, 119, 129, 135*
oysters   *47*

P

***panko* bread crumbs**   *47, 49,* **137**
parsley   *53, 75, 77, 105, 129*
parsnip   *45, 87*
peanut butter   *17, 19, 23, 63, 93*
peanuts   *19, 63*
ponzu sauce   *93*
pork   *35, 49, 73, 135*
potato(es)   *63, 71, 85, 97, 135*

R

rice   *98, 101, 103, 105, 107, 109, 111, 113, 115, 117, 126*
rice vinegar   *126,* **137**

S

sake **138**
salmon   *31, 67, 97*
scallion(s)   *23, 29, 55, 57, 61, 71, 85, 95, 101, 103, 107, 109, 113, 115, 119, 121, 123, 125, 131, 133*
sesami dressing   *24, 49*
sesami seeds   *15, 21, 23, 24, 57, 83, 85, 87, 103, 109, 111, 113, 115, 117*
***shichimi* spice powder**   *29, 33, 79, 95, 107, 121, 123, 125, 131,* **138**
***shiitake* mushrooms**   *33, 65, 67, 87, 91, 93, 97, 103,* **138**
shirataki   *91,* **138**
***shiso* leaves**   *109,* **138**
shrimp   *43, 65, 111, 113*
smoked salmon   *105, 111, 113*
snow peas   *67, 87*

***soba* buckwheat noodles**   *119, 121, 123,* **138**
soy sauce   **138**
spinach   *19, 91, 95*
sprouts   *23, 101, 105, 119*
sukiyaki sauce   *91*
sushi rice   *111, 113, 126*
sushi vinegar   *126*

T

tempura   *43,* **138**
tempura dipping sauce   *43, 45, 58*
teriyaki   *27, 29, 31, 33, 35,* **139**
tobiko   *113*
tofu   *17, 29, 55, 67, 91, 93, 131,* **139**
tomato(es)   *35, 91*
tuna   *101, 111, 113*

U

udon noodles   *125*
umami   **139**

W

wasabi   *101, 111, 113,* **139**
wasabi-mayo sauce   *24, 47*
wasabi-soy dressing   *21*
Worcestershire sauce   *24, 47, 49*

Y

yaki-tofu   *91,* **139**

さくいん

太字のものは食材メモ（pp.136〜139）に説明あり。

あ
あさり　*61, 133*
アナハイム・ペッパー　*29,* **136**
油揚げ　*123,* **136**
アボカド　*111, 113*

い
いか　*79*
いくら　*111, 113,* **136**
いんげん　*15, 63, 79, 97*

う
ウスターソース　*24, 47, 49*
うどん　*125*
うま味　**139**

え
えのき　*67, 93, 97,* **136**
海老　*43, 65, 111, 113*

か
かいわれ　*23, 101, 105, 119*
かき　*47*
かつおぶし　*29, 39, 68, 109, 119, 123,* **136**
かにかまぼこ　*21,* **137**
かぼちゃ　*45, 63, 75,* **137**
かまぼこ　*21,* **137**

き
キャベツ　*35, 49, 97*
牛肉　*27, 71, 91, 93, 125*
きゅうり　*111*
きんぴら　*83, 85,* **137**

く
グリーンピース　*71*

こ
ご飯　*98, 101, 103, 105, 107, 109, 111, 113, 115, 117, 126*
ごぼう　*45, 83, 87*
ごま　*15, 21, 23, 24, 57, 83, 85, 87, 103, 109, 111, 113, 115, 117*
ごまだれ　*24, 49*
米酢　*126,* **137**
コリアンダー　*109*
こんにゃく　**137**
昆布　*67, 68,* **137**

さ
酒　**138**
鮭　*31, 67, 97*
さば　*81*
さやえんどう　*67, 87*

し
しいたけ　*33, 65, 67, 87, 91, 93, 97, 103,* **138**
しそ　*109,* **138**
七味唐辛子　*29, 33, 79, 95, 107, 121, 123, 125, 131,* **138**
じゃがいも　*63, 71, 85, 97, 135*
しょうが　*35, 39, 51, 55, 58, 61, 81, 95, 103, 109, 111*
醤油　**138**
白滝　*91,* **138**

す
すき焼きのたれ　*91*
寿司酢　*126*
寿司飯　*111, 113, 126*
スモークサーモン　*105, 111, 113*

せ
セロリ　*21, 131*

そ
そば　*119, 121, 123,* **138**
空豆　*17*

た
大根　*21, 37, 55, 58, 79, 101,* **136**

だし　68, 88, **136**
卵　37, 43, 47, 49, 51, 65, 95, 107, 109, 111, 113, 129
たまねぎ　23, 33, 57, 91, 105, 107, 111, 113, 119, 129, 135
たら　53

ち
チャービル　45, 65

て
照り焼き　27, 29, 31, 33, 35, **139**
天つゆ　43, 45, 58
天ぷら　43, **138**

と
唐辛子　29, 33, 55, 57, 65, 79, 83, 85, 95, 107, 121, 123, 125, 131, 135
豆腐　17, 29, 55, 67, 91, 93, 131, **139**
とびこ　113
トマト　35, 91
ドライトマト　88
鶏肉　33, 51, 57, 65, 77, 87, 88, 95, 103, 107, 121, 123, 125, 131

な
長ねぎ　33, 91
なす　39
南蛮漬け　57, **136**

に
にら　95
にんじん　45, 57, 63, 83, 87, 93, 131, 135

は
白菜　73, 95
パースニップ　45, 87
パセリ　53, 75, 77, 105, 129
バター　31, 97, 105
パン粉　47, 49, **137**

ひ
ピーナツ　19, 63
ピーナツバター　17, 19, 23, 63, 93

ピーマン　33, 53

ふ
豚肉　35, 49, 73, 135
ブロッコリー　27

へ
ベーコン　23, 73, 75, 85, 117, 129
ベビーリーフ　23, 27

ほ
ほうれん草　19, 91, 95
細ねぎ　23, 29, 55, 57, 61, 71, 85, 95, 101, 103, 107, 109, 113, 115, 119, 121, 123, 125, 131, 133
ポン酢だれ　93

ま
まぐろ　101, 111, 113
マッシュルーム　67, 103

み
味噌　97, 133, 135, **137**
みつば　65

や
焼き豆腐　91, **139**

れ
レタス　47, 53, 93, 103, 111, 113
レモン　21, 23, 27, 31, 47, 51, 53, 57, 65, 67, 73, 77, 93, 103, 111, 117
れんこん　87

わ
わさび　101, 111, 113, **139**
わさびマヨネーズ　24, 47
わさび醤油だれ　21

The author and publisher would like to thank Chisako Hori
and Masahito Tsuji of Kikunoi for their gracious cooperation.

Contributing Editor: Noriko Yokota/Junko Kawakami
Translation: Derek Wilcox/Kirsten McIvor
Copyediting: Katherine Heins/Matthew Cotterill
Proofreading: Yoshiko Ohtaki

英語でかんたん和食
Japanese Home Cooking with Master Chef Murata

2011年3月29日　第 1 刷発行
2025年2月10日　第12刷発行

著　者	村田吉弘
撮　影	齋藤 明
発行者	清田則子
発行所	株式会社講談社
	〒112-8001　東京都文京区音羽 2-12-21
	販売　東京03-5395-5817
	業務　東京03-5395-3615
編　集	株式会社講談社エディトリアル
	代表　堺 公江
	〒112-0013　東京都文京区音羽 1-17-18　護国寺SIAビル
	編集部　東京03-5319-2171
印刷・製本所	大日本印刷株式会社

KODANSHA

落丁本・乱丁本は購入書店名を明記のうえ、講談社業務宛にお送りください。送料小社負担に
てお取り替えいたします。なお、この本についてのお問い合わせは、講談社エディトリアル宛
にお願いいたします。本書のコピー、スキャン、デジタル化等の無断複製は著作権法上での
例外を除き禁じられています。本書を代行業者等の第三者に依頼してスキャンやデジタル化す
ることはたとえ個人や家庭内の利用でも著作権法違反です。

定価はカバーに表示してあります。

©村田吉弘 2011

Printed in Japan
ISBN 978-4-7700-4136-4